CRIMINAL YOUTH
AND THE BORSTAL SYSTEM

CRIMINAL YOUTH

AND THE

BORSTAL SYSTEM

WILLIAM HEALY, M.D.

BENEDICT S. ALPER

NEW YORK · THE COMMONWEALTH FUND

London · Humphrey Milford · Oxford University Press

1941

FOREWORD

THE purpose of this book is to awaken interest in the practical possibilities of more effective methods of dealing with criminal youth in our country. After outlining the background of prevailing inadequacies and failures, we present a more detailed picture than has heretofore been published of the justly renowned Borstal System.

A first observation in 1929 of this British method of training youthful offenders convinced the senior author of its extraordinary worth. Then in 1938 he made a further study of the Borstal System for the Criminal Justice–Youth Committee of the American Law Institute. The report proved to be very stimulating to discussions of this committee and led to some of the recommendations incorporated in the draft of the model Youth Correction Authority Act, adopted by the Institute in 1940. Desire for more details of operation of the Borstal System led Mr. John D. Rockefeller 3rd to supply funds for an intensive study which was begun in the early summer of 1939 with another visit to England for the purpose. The projected year of intimate work with the Borstal personnel by the junior author was cut short by wartime adjustments—the Borstal Institutions themselves before long were either abandoned or largely converted to other uses.

To the English Prison Commissioners—particularly to Alexander Paterson, Dr. J. C. W. Methven, and R. L. Bradley— we offer hearty thanks for their splendid cooperation in allowing us, at the Home Office and in the institutions themselves, to observe at first hand the organization and operation of the Borstal System. For our courteous reception and much time given to us acknowledgments are due the governors and other members of the staffs of the institutions. We regret that their number precludes our naming these devoted public servants, whose personalities in many instances impressed us deeply. The Director of the Borstal Association, Henry Scott, and the Deputy, J. T. Cunliffe, also kindly gave us much assistance. Even in the early trying weeks of the war all those still at their work showed unflagging interest in our inquiries.

To the Judge Baker Research Fund we are indebted for a considerable amount of the time of the senior author and of Dr. Augusta F. Bronner whose aid in the work abroad and in the preparation of this manuscript has been invaluable.

Finally, we express appreciation to the Commonwealth Fund, which gave generous aid to the American Law Institute for the work of the Criminal Justice–Youth Committee and has shown a helpful interest in the publishing of this book.

Judge Baker Guidance Center, Boston W. H.
June, 1940 B. S. A.

CRIMINAL JUSTICE–YOUTH COMMITTEE
OF THE AMERICAN LAW INSTITUTE

WILLIAM DRAPER LEWIS, Philadelphia, *Director of the Institute*
JOHN B. WAITE, Law School, University of Michigan, *Reporter*

CURTIS BOK, Court of Common Pleas, Philadelphia
E. R. CASS, American Prison Association, New York
SHELDON GLUECK, Law School, Harvard University
LEONARD V. HARRISON, Community Service Society, New York
WILLIAM HEALY, M.D., Judge Baker Guidance Center, Boston
EDWIN R. KEEDY, Law School, University of Pennsylvania
AUSTIN H. MACCORMICK, former Commissioner of Corrections, New York City
WILLIAM E. MIKELL, Law School, University of Pennsylvania
THORSTEN SELLIN, Department of Sociology, University of Pennsylvania
JOSEPH N. ULMAN, Supreme Court of Baltimore City

CONTENTS

PART ONE

THE CHALLENGE

CHAPTER I

CRIME IN YOUTH

MUST we continue our amazingly ineffective methods of dealing with youthful offenders?

In this country ever since 1876 the idea of reformatory treatment for younger criminals has been held in principle. But as a matter of fact, except in name the distinction between "reformatories" and prisons for the most part does not exist. To be sure, commitment of a young offender to the former type of institution has behind it the vague intention of "reforming" him, while sentence to a "house of correction" inflicts a penalty supposed to be desirable from the standpoint of society and sentence to a prison or penitentiary effects a longer period of segregation. All else is blurred in a confusion of aims and concepts, through which it is impossible to trace a consistent philosophy or a continuous thread of integrated treatment based on clearly defined purposes.

Somehow, in spite of many indications to the contrary, the early hope for good results from reformatory treatment has persisted. Recently we began to have incontrovertible evidence of the failures of this system. In 1930 a competent study of one of the supposedly best reformatories showed that about eighty per cent of its graduates commit further offenses. So, in the face of the scientific advances of the past few generations in so many other fields, we very apparently have made little progress in dealing successfully either with the young offender who evidences the possibility of rehabilitation or with the really dangerous young criminal from whom society needs thoroughgoing, prolonged protection. In many instances the offender on his second, third, or twenty-fifth offense is shunted through the same process that failed to control his criminal tendencies after he was first taken into custody.

Outstanding general considerations are the following:

Beginning at 16 and 17 years there is a tremendous rise in the commission of criminal offenses. At 19 and 20 more major crimes are committed than at any other age. It is during youth that criminal careers mainly begin.

Youth is a period of special urges and needs, and obviously of new modes of behavior. It is a time when the individual, still an adolescent, is specially susceptible to influences, arising from within or from without himself, which may lead to criminality. These later adolescent years represent a highly formative period in the development of character and conduct tendencies.

Society should, therefore, be aware not only of a great need but also of a great opportunity for dealing with youthful offenders in order to reduce the likelihood of their future criminality. As the matter stands, treatment given youthful offenders under the prescriptions of the law largely fails to prevent repetition of offenses.

While we as a people are known for our efficiency in science, business, and industry, in this matter of dealing with a certain class of human beings who can readily be brought under control, we remain extraordinarily inefficient. If we use good business sense we must face the hard facts of huge monetary costs; if we awaken our social consciousness or conscience we must deplore the unhappiness, anxieties, and wasted years of life—all the products of criminal behavior.

Our present practice must be brought to conform in much greater measure to our accumulated knowledge of the problem as a whole and of the nature and needs of youthful offenders as they are studied and known. Only by these means will it be possible to deal more effectively with the young criminal and more surely to safeguard society.

Are more effective methods of dealing with youthful offenders possible? Are they in operation anywhere? If so, are such methods likely to be of service to this country? To these questions a strongly affirmative answer can be given. Indeed, the source of inspiration for this publication has been our intimate observation of what was being accomplished for the reformation of youthful lawbreakers in other countries, and more particularly in England.

In order to assess the values for us of a system of dealing with young offenders which is rational and has been in large measure successful abroad, it is necessary to have in mind as a background the main features of the problem as it exists in our own country.

Some Facts

From various sources much information can be derived which bears upon the extent, the repetition, and the types of youthful criminality in the United States. For us here merely a few illustrative figures will suffice.*

The Federal Bureau of Investigation received during

* Some of these figures and tables are taken from Thorsten Sellin's admirable compilation of data for the Criminal Justice-Youth Committee.

1939 fingerprints of persons under 21 years of age arrested by police authorities as follows:

Males	101,604
Females	7,253

That this proportion of the total arrests (576,920)
does not vary greatly from year to year is shown by the
following percentages of all persons under 21 finger-
printed and reported to the Federal Bureau of Investigation:

1936	17.4 per cent
1937	18.0 per cent
1938	18.8 per cent
1939	18.9 per cent

Even this does not represent the entire number of
youths arrested because not all law-enforcement officers
in this country report to the Federal Bureau of Investigation and because some officials are loath to fingerprint
youthful offenders.

The United States Census Bureau reports for the year
1937 the males under 21 years of age received from
courts in federal and state prisons and reformatories
(jails and houses of correction not included):

Under 15	39
15 to 17	2,785
18	2,748
19	3,098
20	2,921
Total	11,591

To almost all so-called reformatories offenders above
21 years of age are committed in considerable numbers
but the Pontiac Branch of the Illinois State Peniten-

tiaries, formerly called the Pontiac Reformatory, is an institution for offenders under 21 years. In this institution at the end of 1938 there were no less than 2,642 prisoners, chiefly housed in three cell blocks, generally with two prisoners in each cell. During 1938 the admissions were 906, which made an increase of 566 above the population at the end of the previous year.

Among the defendants in magistrate courts in New York City in 1936, excluding traffic violators, were 19,196 youths.

The arrests in Boston in 1937 included 4,061 youths, 17 to 20 years of age, inclusive.

Of course these figures represent such diverse types of facts that they cannot be used for making comparisons. They merely serve to illustrate the extent of criminality among youth.

The quick rise in criminality at 16 and 17 years is partially indicated by the following ratios of arrests, judged by fingerprint records, per 100,000 males of the same age in the general population, 1935–1937:

Age	Ratio
16	1,412.3
17	2,120.8
18	2,547.4
19	2,681.6
20	2,379.2
21	2,406.3

The study of 1,000 admissions to Elmira Reformatory, 1935–1936, by Dr. Breguet,[1] shows the following

1. R. Breguet, Amer. Jour. of Medical Jurisprudence, Oct., 1938.

ages at admission (here we must remember that in the State of New York the jurisdiction of the juvenile court ceases at 16 years):

Age	Per cent of admissions
16	6.4
17	9.0
18	14.9
19	17.6
20	15.3
21	11.0

The remarkable acceleration of criminalistic behavior in the last years of the "teen ages" is also evidenced by the Uniform Crime Reports of the Federal Bureau of Investigation. Notable, too, is the fact that the total arrests per age reach a very early maximum and show an appreciable drop before the age of 25. For example, in 1939, as in some previous years, the nineteen-year-old group showed the largest number of arrests.

Age	Arrests
16	11,593
17	17,947
18	24,225
19	25,191
20	21,398
21	23,788
22	24,007
23	23,092
24	22,464

The next point to consider is the nature of the offenses committed by youth. It must not be concluded from the above data that the greatest number of arrests or convictions for lawbreaking of any kind falls within the youth period. When totals include such offenses as drunkenness, vagrancy, disorderly conduct, and traffic violations, "which together comprise four-fifths of the transgressions of the law," the next older age period of five years, 21 to 25 inclusive, rates higher. But serious crimes of several sorts are particularly those of youth. At this age a high proportion of burglaries, larcenies, and robberies are committed.

This is clearly demonstrated by the following table which shows the ratio of arrests of males for major offenses to every 100,000 males of the same age in the United States during the years 1935 to 1937 (the figure in italics is the highest ratio for *any age*).

	Age in years						
Offense	*16*	*17*	*18*	*19*	*20*	*21*	*22*
Robbery	73	139	207	249	246	249	253
Burglary	486	649	*680*	636	513	477	446
Larceny	476	719	822	*835*	701	692	756
Auto theft	208	300	*347*	319	234	212	195
Total	1,412	2,120	2,547	*2,681*	2,379	2,406	2,501

In Massachusetts in 1935 the youth group (16 to 21 years old) was responsible for 38.7 per cent of all "offenses against property with violence" and 22.9 per cent of all "offenses against property without violence."

Among the 1,000 admissions to Elmira, mentioned above, were commitments for offenses as follows:

Burglary .   .   .   . 32.5 per cent
Robbery .   .   .   . 29.4 per cent
Grand larceny   .   . 17.3 per cent

Of all those arrested and reported to the Federal Bureau of Investigation during 1939 for robbery, bur-

glary, larceny, and auto theft (125,574) 38.1 per cent
or 47,891 were under 21 years of age.

The scheme of classification of the census and the
Uniform Crime Reports makes it possible to compare
the following four-year age groups for 1939:

| Offense | Age in years | |
	17–20	21–24
Robbery	3,435	3,399
Burglary	11,857	6,634
Larceny	16,272	11,086
Auto theft	4,945	2,548
Total	36,509	23,667

The tendency to repetition of offense (recidivism) on
the part of individuals in the youth group can be readily
indicated.

At Elmira the median age at commitment is 20 years.
In 1932 some 79 per cent had known criminal records
prior to the offenses for which they were committed, and
45 per cent had earlier served in correctional institutions. In 1935–1936 we find that in 74 per cent of the
admissions the age was 21 or less and that the records
showed commitment on first arrest for only one quarter
of the cases. Indeed the average number of known arrests was three, with a range from 1 to 19 arrests. Of
course this can only mean that a great majority had previously run afoul of the law during the youth period.

In 1938 some 1,800 prisoners who were known to
have had criminal records prior to the offense for which
they had just served sentence were released on parole in
the State of New York. Of these, 1,197 had been arrested for earlier offenses at least once before they were

CRIME IN YOUTH   II

21. Judging by the Elmira figures many must have had
additional arrests before the age of 21.

It is a curious fact that with one exception there seem
to be no exact studies of recidivism among those who
have been dealt with by the law when they were youthful offenders. The outstanding exception is the research
by the Gluecks concerning 510 inmates of the Massachusetts Reformatory at Concord.[2] Since this is probably
a typical correctional institution for younger offenders,
dealing with a typical section of our American population, the findings of the Gluecks can be accepted with
very considerable confidence as representative.

The average age of these 510 reformatory inmates
was 20 years at the time of commitment. Only 9 per cent
had no earlier record of offenses. Previously 56 per cent
had been committed to penal or correctional institutions
and the average age at first commitment was seventeen
years, six months. Already there was evidence that treatment given these offenders during the youth period had
done little or nothing to curb their criminal propensities.

Since many of the above, 60 per cent, were receiving
reformatory treatment before the age of 21 (34 per cent
had been committed to Concord at 18 years or younger),
it is important for us here to note the results as ascer-
tained by the Gluecks' follow-up studies. They found
that during five years subsequent to parole from Concord practically 80 per cent of the 422 whose conduct
record could be traced were again offenders and 44 per
cent committed such serious crimes that they again were

2. Sheldon and Eleanor Glueck, *500 Criminal Careers*, 1930, and
Later Criminal Careers, 1937.

sentenced to penal institutions for an average term of twenty-two months.

In a study of the same group for a further period of five years it was found that among 200 known to have been again arrested, 111 were newly committed, with an average sentence of twenty-four months. Of those who were again offenders during the second five-year period, 136 (68 per cent) were 21 years of age or under at the time of the original commitment to Concord Reformatory.

CHAPTER II

THE OLDER ADOLESCENT AND CRIME

THE tremendous upsurge of criminality during the youth period is a startling social phenomenon. No other age shows any such marked and rapid change in behavior tendencies. The facts indicate that new and special processes are active in human lives, that special causations are directing conduct trends.

Considered in general, youth presents unique problems. The characteristics and life situations of the age group 16 to 21 years are sharply differentiated in several particulars from those of younger adolescents who, together with children, form the group properly designated as juveniles. Also, for the reasons given below, there are a number of important differences between behavior tendencies and environmental situations at this age and those that belong typically to full adult life, whether one considers it is reached at 21, 23, or 25 years.

First, the physical changes that occur between early adolescence and manhood are those of continued rapid growth in the framework of the body, the stature, and particularly the size of the organs and muscles. These changes are so great that at 20 years of age the individual frequently bears little resemblance in features and build to the boy that he was at 15 years. And when we occasionally find a lad of 16 who because of his appearance could pass for 21 or 22, we instantly recognize him as anomalous in growth characteristics and as having obvious, definite, social liabilities.

Then the complexity of the growth process, often with discrepancies in the relative increase of size and functioning of different parts of the body, has its hazards, inasmuch as it may lead the youth to feel insecure and confused about himself and his relationship to the world. With all the physiological alterations that are going on, sometimes poorly balanced one with another, it is no wonder that youth finds itself experiencing moods and impulses that are difficult to control.

The heightened activity of the glands of internal secretion, with their effect not only upon other bodily organs but upon each other, and also the possibilities of imbalance in the functioning of these glands—all of which has been so well demonstrated by recent scientific investigations—can easily lead to disturbed feelings and unstable emotional attitudes. From such physical sources new urges, new feelings of restlessness and impatience, resulting in reckless behavior, are fairly common to youth and may be largely responsible in some cases for the exhibition of antisocial conduct. We find that many an adult, speaking of earlier offenses, says that he acted in such foolish ways because those were the years when he was so unstable and impulsive.

Anyone with much experience in studying youthful offenders is aware that, considered from a psychological standpoint, youth is a period, not only of instability, but often of real confusion of ideas and emotions. The young man, for we commonly so designate him, may frankly say that he does not know what to make of his feelings and urges or what to do about himself. Not infrequently someone of this age in straightforward fashion asks for the discipline and restraint that army or navy life affords, just because he feels that he cannot manage himself. Then quite apart from actual insanity, one notes occasional cases in which the confused mental states strongly suggest a mild psychosis.

Of course, with various modifications during the period of youth, there is continuance of many of the emotional attitudes, dissatisfactions, conflicts, and ideas of earlier years, and the continuance of behavior tendencies already established. Then the family interrelationships and the more general environmental circumstances, either or both of which may have had much influence on the development of antisocial conduct, frequently have been little altered. But with increase of physical vigor and urge to action there is release of feelings of aggressiveness and decrease of feelings of fear.

Now parental admonitions and restrictions can be defied and chances taken with the authorities of society. There is now real pleasure in adventure and in the reckless and even violent deed. The dependent age of childhood with its normal fears—and perhaps its milder misdeeds—is followed by a period when the desire for emancipation from restraints and rules appears. There is need for proving oneself by doing something new and different. The individual feels thwarted in his urges and wants to grow up, having the idea that manhood largely means doing as one pleases.

This evolution can be traced in thousands of cases where the beginning or the accentuation of lawbreaking tendencies is to be observed at about sixteen years of age. The induction of boys into criminal gangs is well known as a phenomenon of response to social pressures, but also to be noted is the response to the inner urge to reckless activity in combination with the acceptance of a boyish notion of what constitutes definite proof of virility. Perhaps no better example can be given than that of the exploits of the "loop-the-loopers" in Charlestown, Massachusetts. For so many years have there been severe outbreaks of this criminal activity that it has become almost a local tradition. And this in spite of the terrific accidents, injuries, deaths, and prison sentences that have resulted time and again. Looping-the-loop means to drive a stolen car up Bunker Hill and down again at such high speed that the police will be afraid to intercept it. Often the young people of the vicinity have been previously apprised of the escapade so that they will be on the look-out to witness it. The police have taken great pains to prevent this dangerous exhibitionism, even placing barriers on the street; the game then being for the driver to avoid these. Boys of this locality have revealed that at one time there existed scales or grades of achievement leading up to this highest criminal exploit. The lowest grade of misdoing was "fishing cars," namely, stealing articles from parked cars, and the next was taking a ride in a car stolen by others. Then came the actual taking of a car for a "joy ride," and, finally, the highest rank was given to those who would drive a stolen car over the loop. Naturally, the last two more desperate forms of criminality were entered into only by the older youths.

But the ideas and impulses and the surcharged emotions of youth that tend to bring about antisocial conduct are not merely dependent on what goes on within the individual. Social situations arise that are peculiar to the period between childhood and adult life. With release from school at about sixteen, which is the history common to most offenders nowadays, many old companionships are broken and the boy finds himself more or less adrift and free to associate with casual acquaintances or perchance with older fellows whose behavior tendencies are unsettled. His increase of vigor and instability and his new liberties readily permit association with other restive and dissatisfied youths who are willing to embark upon criminal adventure. Or being adrift socially, the individual, from any of the many sources that suggest profits of crime, may in a confusion of ideas seize upon criminality as offering a solution for his own disturbing uncertainties.

The responsibilities and restraints that are the natural accompaniments of maturity are in youth not yet felt to be inhibiting forces. Perhaps realization that the age of legal responsibility in financial matters and in civic affairs is not yet reached adds to the feeling of recklessness and irresponsibility. But, on the other hand, perhaps it is "the wisdom of the ages" that has led to such appreciation of the import of the biological and psychological phenomena of youth that full responsibility is not legally invoked until the twenty-first birthday. Anyhow the latter is the age at which recklessness as judged by criminal statistics begins to decline.

There is still another matter which in our national

life has bearing upon the development of criminal pro-
clivities during youth. Phrased most easily it is the problem of occupation. From 16 to 21 years is the period
of greatest vocational maladjustment. The youth is of
working age; very frequently indeed what he has
learned of vocational importance in the school he cannot
utilize in finding a job; very few chances are offered for
working as an apprentice—perhaps one of the faults of
our times; employment opportunities are for the most
part casual and temporary; unemployment is common.
Thus to the natural instability of this period of life are
added only too definite economic and vocational uncertainties. In other countries where trades and occupations
are entered into from the more settled and secure basis
of an apprenticeship system, even though wage scales are
lower and beginnings are slower, the feeling of security
and of recognition for workmanship, from what we have
observed, plays no small part in deterring youth from
antisocial conduct. In America the chance that a youth
may on occasion make "good money" for a short time,
often as good wages as an adult of experience, spoils him
for steadier employment on smaller wages and leaves
him, in his years of irresponsibility and suggestibility,
very open to thoughts of how "easy money" is to be obtained in illicit ways.

Then, finally, any realistic observer of the causes for
the accentuation of criminalism during youth learns that
through new experiences the individual often builds up
an attitude of cynicism concerning honesty and whether
it pays. Recreational contacts in pool rooms or gambling
places and the like, or connection with some aspects of

business or even of political life may have produced this unfortunate attitude. The youth finds his activities and doings part of our whole social structure as he never did while attending school. In the confusions and uncertainties of the youth period, the more malignant phases of social life are easily interpreted as being normal, excusable, and thoroughly remunerative. Evidently there is a game that is played and the youth thinks he will take a chance at it.

This sketch of the older adolescent could have every detail drawn with precision from our clinical case studies. From such a picture can be learned something of the treatment methods necessary for the reorientation of young offenders. And in planning treatment the most encouraging consideration is to be found in the fact that youth is still predominantly a formative age—flexibility and suggestibility have not yet been replaced by the more crystallized patterns of adult behavior. Wisely directed efforts to reconstruct standards of conduct during youth cannot fail to have a considerable chance of being successful.

CHAPTER III

CLINICAL EXAMPLES OF YOUTHFUL OFFENDERS

THE diversity of problems presented by older adolescent offenders may be made more vivid by giving a few examples. These have been chosen in order to show, on the one hand, some of the ineptitudes and inefficiencies of the ordinary methods of dealing with such cases and, on the other, some of the possibilities of effective treatment after the individual and his whole life situation have been studied and taken into account.

These eight cases selected from the clinical records of the Judge Baker Guidance Center of course by no means represent the range of individual needs for treatment in reformatory institutions. The conclusions to be drawn from any one case are not so important for our purposes as the picture of the complexities in both motivation and behavior revealed by the histories of these young men. But even in these few instances, from among the hundreds that we could cite, we see exemplifications of the fact that the usual commitment to correctional institutions often does little to assure protection of the public from socially dangerous individuals. Nor does commitment to a reformatory, save in exceptional instances, offer the least promise of the highly individualized interest and professionally guided assistance which is the necessary foundation for changing the course of the lives of the great number who obviously need very special forms of treatment.

The case of A is that of a well-endowed youth whose early and later difficulties were not met by any therapeutic measures aimed at correcting his underlying problems. The latter very evidently were of the type that lead young men to join the army of aimless vagabonds who, succumbing to immature impulses, constantly seek new experiences as an escape from deep feelings of frustration which are untouched by institutional life and are not solved or alleviated by their wanderings.

When A was fifteen years old he left his home in Massachusetts and made his way to Colorado and Utah. He had run away on twenty previous occasions, the first time when he was eleven years old, being gone as long as two or three weeks at a time. The police had picked him up in various places and he had appeared in several juvenile courts. On his last appearance, the court sent him to a correctional school to which seriously delinquent boys are committed.

Clinical examination on one occasion revealed that A was in fair physical condition and showed very good mental abilities of various sorts. The psychiatrist found the boy extremely unhappy, with much inner conflict about several matters, including association with bad companions, sexual experiences, and a feeling that he was rejected by his parents. The latter was true; his father had refused to take him home and had asked in court that his son be sent away. The golden opportunity for doing psychotherapy or other constructive work for the boy, now sixteen, was lost when he was sent to the correctional school. Upon his release, he speedily ran away again.

When he was seventeen and wandering through the West, he was arrested for burglary in the nighttime and sent to a state reformatory, which, from the standpoint of bricks and mortar and work program, is one of the best in the United States. He was treated in formal routine fashion and made a very good record within the institution. He was paroled at the age of eighteen without any therapeutic plan being made for him. He again began his roaming and was killed while trespassing on a railroad.

~

A series of short-term sentences to correctional institutions is the lot of many of our youthful offenders who repeatedly engage in misdemeanors or minor felonies. The application of such piecemeal measures in the cases of young men who are plainly in need of a really constructive and continuing scheme of treatment is bound to result in failure. Such sentences are nothing less than frivolous, wasteful, and even dangerous in such a case as the following, where a mentally defective criminal was not segregated over long years, as he should have been, for the safe protection of society. Moreover, even in such a case there is the possibility that prolonged training may lead to the formation of new habits and attitudes that will offset to a considerable degree already developed antisocial conduct tendencies.

During his seventeenth year B appeared in court five times charged with larceny, assault, threats, and public profanity. On each occasion he was given either a suspended sentence to an institution or a term of probation.

His earlier record in juvenile courts included offenses of larceny, participation in a gang attack upon a store-keeper, and theft of a large quantity of wine. Here, too, he had been either placed on probation or given a suspended sentence. When he was fourteen he had been diagnosed as "Moron, I.Q. 71, with some suggestions of being mentally unbalanced." He was reported to have suffered in the past from convulsions and various other ailments. He came from a family of poor heredity in which there had been much delinquency. His home life was marked by poverty and very poor parental supervision. He admitted that he had been heavily engaged in sex affairs.

Between the ages of sixteen and twenty-five, B appeared in court twenty-nine times, not counting separate charges or court continuances. His sentences were always either small fines, probation, or short commitments of fourteen days, one month, or two months in the house of correction. Appeals to the superior court not infrequently resulted in the filing of his case. When he was twenty-two, he was held for one year at the state farm. Within two years, he was given another sentence to the state farm, which was suspended. Allowed to go free, within a month he again appeared in court after a severe accident in which he had been the drunken driver. His court appearances continued—for being drunk, for violating city ordinances, and for assault.

B is now thirty-five years old. During the past ten years he has been in court for a total of twenty-four separate offenses. Six charges have been for non-support of his family and six for larceny; the other offenses have included assault, operating an automobile under the influence of liquor, and drunkenness. In these later years he has either been fined, given a suspended sentence, or committed (seven times) for terms no longer than six months in the house of correction. During this period also he has sometimes avoided serving sentences through appeals. The number of offenses charged against him to date totals sixty-seven.

～

The hardened young offender, cynical beyond his years, seemingly immune to any feelings of remorse, presents a most difficult challenge to any institutional officer. He gives every outward evidence of being unyielding, and is taken at his face value by those who provide him with custody and a fixed, daily regime. Experienced officials are not too sanguine about his attitudes being thus reformed. However, conformity to the regime is sometimes presumed to indicate an inner change, despite the obvious fact that his real outlook on life has not been appraised nor his feelings about himself and the world understood or redirected. The possibilities of successful psychotherapeutic treatment of some such young men are indicated by the following brief summary.

C appeared in court when nearly seventeen on two charges of robbery with a gun. At the same time he was wanted in another court for a similar offense.

Opportunity was presented for a thorough clinical study. Investigation revealed that C had come from a southwestern family of pioneering stock, a hardy lot who in an isolated primitive environment freely indulged in alcohol, sex immorality, and fighting. The boy had been deserted by his own mother, later by his father and his father's paramours. With an attractive personality, of athletic adult build, and with strong features, he demonstrated on tests decidedly good mental abilities. However, it was found that in attitudes he was mature, hard, and materialistic, rejecting any code of honor. He had grown to have many criminalistic ideas and much cynicism about the world. He evidently sensed his capacities and his present plan of life was to "get away" with all he could. At the clinic he confessed that earlier in a midwestern city he had been engaged in systematic stealing with a gang of young men who had netted considerable sums of money in this way. He had not been apprehended for any of these offenses.

Upon receiving our report of the boy's potentialities and his immediate response to the idea of being helped, both courts, in spite of his serious delinquencies, agreed to a trial period of psychotherapeutic reeducation for him, provided he could be placed in a good home. They wisely agreed that a sentence to a reformatory would probably embitter and further harden him. A child-placing agency consented to enter into the experiment although the boy was beyond their usual age limit. They discovered a home where he would be accepted in the family circle. C soon responded well in interviews with a psychiatrist; together they explored the foundations of his antisocial attitudes. As his emotional tensions were released, he gained insight into the futility of his hostilities and in line with his capabilities developed ambitions which he followed with steadfastness. For a long time

he continued friendly contacts with the psychiatrist, and
in these and in his relationships with the foster family
he found the anchorage of which life previously had deprived him. He is now twenty-six years old. During the
intervening period there has been no recurrence of criminal conduct. His whole outlook on life has undergone a
complete change; he has worked hard, saved his money,
educated himself in preparation for a career, made good
friends, and is now studying in a graduate school.

The cooperation of the offender in the application of
a plan of treatment is, of course, a prerequisite to any
successful outcome. In the following case the desire to
cooperate has been amply demonstrated. D himself long
ago begged for psychiatric aid, and still continues to do
so, but despite long periods of confinement he has never
yet received the kind of help he seeks. His conformity
to the requirements of the regime at the dozen or more
institutions in which he has served sentences has most
often mistakenly seemed to indicate that he did not require the continued attention of a psychiatrist. Even
when, as in some institutions, there has been realization
through the history of the case that D, an unusually capable young man, is subject to irrational compulsions,
there has not been a specialist available nor has it been
possible under the existing penal regulations to transfer
him to any other institution for the prolonged psychotherapy that his case requires.

D was almost seventeen when he appeared in court
charged with larceny. He asked to be sent to the adult

reformatory because, he declared, he had already been committed four times to juvenile correctional institutions and that what he needed was more severe punishment. He had been thieving at intervals since he was nine or ten years old; he could give no excuse for it and said that somehow he felt an urge to steal. His family were of excellent standing in the community and lived in comfortable circumstances.

D has strong features, a very direct, pleasant expression, and a splendid physique. Tests have demonstrated not only his good average mental ability but also his exceptional language and reasoning powers. He always gives the impression of being ingenuous, truthful, sincere, and likable. Committed at sixteen by the court to the reformatory for adults, he made a consistently good record, as he always has done while in institutions. After an early release on parole he engaged in further criminal activity of the same type, and when again apprehended began his requests for psychotherapeutic treatment which has never been available to him.

Up to the present time, D, now thirty-five years old, has been in ten or twelve different state and federal prisons where he has always behaved extremely well. He has endeared himself to various prison officials by his industry, good conduct, and fine personality qualities. On one occasion while within an institution he was cited for heroism at a time of danger. Sometimes on parole he has worked excellently at his job until his compulsion again overtook him. He is married and has several children, but at times has run away from his family to engage in more criminality, even when he was earning well. During all these years he has pitifully sought for the individual help through psychotherapy which he properly conceives will offer the most promise. His family also greatly desire such aid for him. At present he is in an institution with warrants out against him for breaking parole in several states. He has never shown any signs of deterioration and remains the same active, strong personality, optimistic about the possibility of cure through the bringing to light of the deep origins of his totally irrational career.

The lack of any wise, farseeing plan of dealing with an abnormal personality who exhibits criminal tendencies is apparent in the case which follows. The impending difficulties were seen early and could have been avoided by some form of appropriate segregation over the years. One may hope that some day experimental re-educative treatment will be tried in such cases. At any rate society has the right and the duty to prevent such socially disastrous careers.

E, when he was sixteen years old, ran a thousand miles away from home after he had held up some small boys with a gun. Upon his return he was brought to court and placed on probation. His earlier history ran as follows. E had first appeared in the juvenile court at nine years on a charge of breaking, entering, and larceny, but the case had been filed. He was in another juvenile court again at eleven and at this time clinical investigation revealed that he had been seriously delinquent during the preceding two years, stealing bicycles, breaking into buildings, indulging in sex perversions, staying out all night. His mother stated that he was absolutely indifferent to punishment or to police warning or detention.

Observation and the mother's story tended to show that the boy was definitely an abnormal personality, probably on an organic basis. There were several cases of epilepsy in the family but E had not had any attacks. However, at two years he had suffered a severe brain concussion. From that time he had been wilful, uninhibited, and frequently quite unmanageable. His physical development was very good and he demonstrated unusual strength. Psychological tests showed him to have fair mental ability in general, but he gave a very erratic performance. The diagnosis was made that he was a "psychopathic personality"; and since he had exhibited such delinquent tendencies, the necessity for prolonged segregation was emphasized by the clinic. Sent to a correctional school and paroled after the usual brief period, he was returned there two or three times after further delinquencies. Paroled again when he was fifteen, he went to live with relatives in another state. Here he caused a great deal of disturbance in school by his general mischief and fighting. Before long he returned to his home and speedily engaged in the delinquency first mentioned.

After various minor offenses, about which nothing was done, he next appeared in court at the age of eighteen for carrying a revolver. He appealed a six months' sentence and on appeal his case was placed on file. Shortly afterward he was in court on a serious charge of burglary and sentenced for an indefinite term to the reformatory. There he was found extremely difficult and erratic in behavior, constantly losing marks for fighting, disobedience, and violations of regulations. He was nevertheless paroled after fifteen months. When he was twenty-one years old he was convicted of robbery and assault and given a sentence of eight years. Five years later he was again paroled; in less than two years he was convicted of an assault, attempt to murder, and attempt to rape. This time, aged twenty-eight, he was given a sentence of four to six years in the state prison.

The story of F is that of an adolescent with good reason for holding a grudge against society. The boy had received little or no help in adjusting himself to his most difficult social situation; indeed his unremedied personal appearance had led him to be practically ostracized. To be sure, any other case exactly parallel to that of F would be hard to find in these days of good medical care for the children of our cities, but it epitomizes what, in various forms of antisocial attitudes, may result from deeply felt thwartings and rejections.

And then in its outcome the case finely evidences the reconstructive possibilities of intelligent attention given to the individual needs of a reformatory inmate—attention given in this instance by the busy superintendent of a large institution.

F, just before he was seventeen, was arrested for shooting a man who purposely obstructed his way into a building. While F was being held for trial, the wounded man died. The first charge of murder was changed to man-slaughter and F received a sentence of fifteen years. Less than a year before, the boy had appeared in a juvenile court for carrying a revolver. After a week in jail he was placed on probation and advised to go to a skin clinic for his facial disfigurement.

The boy was studied for the purpose of diagnosis just after the homicide. He was found to be normal in general development but his vision was very defective and he possessed no glasses. With his flat features, everted lower eyelids, and an extreme case of facial acne, he was most unattractive and from the way he kept his head always bent over, it was clear that he himself sensed his own re-pulsiveness. On psychological tests he did well, but told his story with a certain amount of mental confusion and with some display of paranoidal ideas. He felt he had been treated badly in many ways—everybody had con-spired to defeat his aims. There was the question of whether or not he was mentally abnormal. In the light of his history which showed much justification for his ideas, the opinion was offered by the clinic that he was not psychotic.

Study of the origin of his social attitudes, which had long been peculiar, brought out the fact that he had suf-fered from his severe skin disease since very young child-hood. On account of it, he had never made friends and even when small had kept very much to himself. He finally became so withdrawn that he stopped going to school, his truancy being excused because he was really not wanted in the classroom. His people were poor, ignorant immigrants who never carried through any treatment plan for him, and the boy, without friends to accompany him, dreaded to venture into clinics.

From the standpoint of remedying his extreme disfigurement, nothing was ever done by anybody. For a couple of years he had been so sensitive about his appearance that he hardly ever ventured out in the daytime, remaining at home and dwelling on his miseries and the possibility of inventing something that would bring renown to him and wealth to his family. The boy had run away once for some three months, but had failed to make a living and had returned home.

It occurred to him that someone might be able to help him with his inventions, and he began writing letters to various people about his fantastic notions. In the meantime he had purchased a revolver with the purpose of doing away with himself if aid for him was not forthcoming. It was in the pursuit of his ideas that he attempted to approach a person of means. In a struggle with a man who blocked his way the revolver was discharged and the man wounded.

In the reformatory F was fortunate enough to elicit the sympathy of the superintendent who singled him out as one in great need of friendliness and treatment. Through this attention, and with skilled medical treatment, he improved much in his attitudes toward the world, no less than in his appearance. He responded splendidly to the sympathetic understanding which had never been afforded him earlier. Paroled after serving ten years, he has since been earning enough to support himself, has not developed a psychosis, and has not been in any further criminality.

~

During mid-adolescence and the years directly follow-ing, the individual may show such exaggerated self-inter-est and such preoccupation with his own urges and impul-sive ideas that he can be easily turned toward the path of criminality. This is especially so when the young person believes himself misunderstood by his family or feels his home life to be too restrictive and in conflict with his de-sires for emancipation. We have known not a few cases in which behavior resultant from such a conflict was the be-ginning of a career of criminality. Since reformatories re-ceive older adolescent offenders with this type of causa-tion looming large as one determinant of their antisocial conduct, there should be professional resources in the in-stitution and during parole treatment to deal intelli-gently with underlying problems of personality and situation. We offer an illustration of what can be accom-plished in a case of this kind.

G, just over sixteen years old, was a big, strong, healthy-appearing boy who could easily pass for nine-teen or twenty. Three times within a year he had run away from home, staying several weeks at a time. On the last trip an adult criminal formed an acquaintance with him and together they had engaged in some holdups and a blackmailing operation which involved a well-to-do homosexual man.

Though he was involved in such serious offenses—for

which the older man was sentenced to prison—the case was referred to the clinic for thorough study. After recommendations were made the court decided to place the boy on probation while treatment was attempted.

Although G had not recently progressed satisfactorily in school, the test results showed average mental ability. Through the history obtained and through interviews with him it came out clearly that G had been experiencing a tremendous adolescent revolt against home restrictions. In connection with the two previous flights from home he had engaged in some dishonesty and had met with some poor companions but only during his last period away had he been so desperately criminal. He appeared terribly sore at heart and unhappy. He seemed to have lost faith in everything and his mind was filled with ideas concerning the possibilities of gains to be derived from criminality. His parents were hard-working, thoroughly honest people, laying great emphasis on religion and having no understanding of the needs of their overgrown adolescent son. The boy's attitude toward the church was particularly bad because the family pastor, having been consulted by the father, advised a sound thrashing which the father, for the first time in the boy's life, administered most thoroughly. Directly following this incident the second running away occurred and the boy's association with bad companions began.

The first steps in the program of treatment were met by a lack of response on the part of the boy. Then he did poorly in an institution where he was placed temporarily for a period of observation. But when a foster home was found for him with outgoing and sympathetic foster parents, he began to improve in his willingness to face the origins of his delinquent behavior. As the result of many psychiatric interviews, frequent at first and continuing for months, he gained insight and changed his emotional attitudes. However, his freer life in a jolly foster home was certainly an important contributing factor that cannot be overlooked in explaining the remarkable change in the boy. Also a considerable part of the accomplishment is traceable to the fact that the attitudes of his parents were modified through the psychiatric work which was done with them. He returned to his home life after eighteen months and in the succeeding seven years has done extremely well, with no relapses into antisocial conduct.

The lack of coordinated aim in court and correctional treatment is only too often apparent in the successive processes by which a young offender is dealt with. In the case of H it seems as if firm handling and appropriate and prolonged training and discipline—all coupled with intelligent attempts to discover and treat the sources of his tendencies to misconduct—might well have prevented his development into a hardened adult criminal.

Between his seventeenth and nineteenth birthdays, H appeared in court fifteen times, sometimes with several charges against him for breaking and entering, stealing automobiles, and excessive speeding. Each time he was either placed on probation or given short sentences—which were appealed and subsequently filed in the upper court—or a small fine.

The records show that H had been in juvenile courts

on eight occasions before he was sixteen years old and given probation until on his last appearance he was committed to a correctional school. Sent for diagnosis to a clinic when he was eleven years old, he had been found to have otorrhea, many carious teeth, and large tonsils. Whether or not these were at all causative of his misbehavior, they were indicative of his neglect. (Presumably these physical conditions were taken care of, at least by the time he was sent to the training school.) He graded as having quite good mental ability and showed no evidences of mental abnormality. Before he went to the training school at fifteen, he had been a member of an extremely lawless gang whose main activity was the commission of offenses. After he returned home on parole, he became the leader of this crowd, and it was learned that he had great influence over them. Reports were that members of his family were able to use political influence to get him off.

By the time he was eighteen, more serious offenses were in evidence. Between then and the age of twenty-seven he appeared in court at least three times for armed robbery, sometimes with several counts against him, besides various charges of larceny of automobiles. He successfully appealed several sentences but was once committed for a short time. He was finally sentenced to the state prison for a term of from fourteen to sixteen years.

Any system of institutional training and treatment or of preventive custody of offenders in the age group from sixteen to twenty-one years must be equipped with proper personnel, men aware of such problems as are outlined in the cases presented above and prepared to attempt to solve them. Proof is given that well-oriented treatment can frequently be effective. In some cases there was evidence of trouble long before the later adolescent years, but juvenile courts or training schools gave little help. It is very true that the reformatories receive the results of early failures as well as those who seem to have been newly recruited to criminal ways. But in either case, there is the challenge to reform these individual offenders while they are still in a formative period of life.

CHAPTER IV

REFORMATORIES TODAY

THE earliest institutions in this country for young offenders, established in the first half of the last century, arose in response to a growing realization that children should be kept apart from older and more hardened criminals, to prevent the contamination which otherwise resulted. In general, these institutions were originally limited to an upper age of fourteen, no doubt out of deference to the common-law precedent that this represented the last year of limited responsibility for criminal acts committed by minors. Special methods were introduced for the training of these juveniles, and emphasis shifted gradually from a philosophy of imprisonment as punishment to a belief in the value of corrective treatment.

The year 1876 saw the establishment of the first reformatory for young offenders above the juvenile level. Here previous notions of punishment were to be supplanted by training and discipline for first offenders from ages eighteen to twenty-five. The idea of an indeterminate sentence to accompany the introduction of reformatory methods unfortunately failed of passage through the New York Legislature, but the advance made by the establishment of Elmira Reformatory was expected to mark a turning point in American methods of dealing with the offender in his late teens and early twenties.

Ably championed by its proponents and skilfully interpreted by its administrators, the principles on which Elmira Reformatory were founded soon came to be looked upon as the nearest to a final answer to the problem of treating youthful criminality that had yet been devised. The very word "reformatory" was applied to a variety of penal and correctional institutions in all sections of the country. Approximately one-half of our states now have one of these institutions as part of their prison programs.

It is important to stress the early basis of the Elmira plan. It was originally intended to be limited to men who were still at an impressionable age—roughly from sixteen to thirty; it was to receive offenders who had never before served a sentence; the term was to be indeterminate to allow men to earn their freedom through a plan of progressive grades which would ultimately see them ready for release; within the institution a strict military regime and a rigorous course of training were to harden them, give them a necessary discipline, and accustom them to the habit of steady work.

With two or three exceptions—including Annandale, one of the best (see p. 49), and in tremendous contrast, Pontiac (see p. 6)—our so-called reformatories are not limited to the younger elements in our criminal population who can, presumably, best respond to reformatory methods. They receive offenders from the ages of fifteen up to thirty or thirty-five, while at least ten such institutions have no upper age limit. The intake at these institutions is not confined to first offenders or to those who have never before served in a penocorrectional institution. While some reformatories have farms where a selected group of men work outside the institution walls when they are deemed ready for less intensive supervision, the

open colony or camp idea for the training of young offenders is almost completely unknown except in juvenile
reformatories.)

The three thousand odd short-term institutions, including county jails, county farms, and houses of correction, are no respecters of youth or of those having no previous criminal history. They receive persons in the age
group sixteen to twenty-one, as well as a motley assort-
ment of sentenced offenders, juveniles on detention,
drunks, material witnesses, appellants, and those who are
awaiting trial or serving out fines. The age group which
commits the largest proportion of serious crimes and
offers the greatest promise of reform may thus be said to
find almost no institution exclusively devoted to its care.

The traditional Philadelphia and Auburn systems
with their individual cells, conditions of maximum security, and the idea of "bigness" have carried down
through the establishment of Elmira to the present day.
We may speak of "mass production" in the treatment of
a large criminal population among our youth inside huge
so-called reformatories. For administrative purposes,
"bigness" has distinct advantages. We have not yet, however, faced the consequences of such mass handling of
individuals. We have built large institutions for our large
number of offenders, and this tradition is hard to break.
Twenty-five reformatories for men in the United States
have an average population of 1,100. The smallest has a
capacity of 200; twelve house over 1,000, while two reformatories accommodate between 2,000 and 3,000, and
two exceed 3,000.

The device of classification has been heralded as providing the solution of the problem created by concentration of these huge numbers of men behind the reformatory walls. Some of these institutions compile the most comprehensive, most carefully verified case histories to be found in any prison system in the world. The value of these studies is largely limited to their use by parole boards. Some of our best reformatories know many important facts about their inmates, and can classify them into finely shaded differentiations. When this is done, they are then at a loss to know how to deal with them; facilities are limited and segregation of the several main groups into separate wings or sections of the institution for living purposes does not prevent their intermingling at work, at meals, during recreation and assembly periods, and in hospitals. Emphasis upon individualization has carried us through the stages of investigation and classification. A penological science of diagnosis has made great advances and awaits now only the time when it may be given the opportunity to experiment with and to apply various treatment methods.

Because of the diverse nature of the criminal elements with which they have to deal, these reformatories are forced to impose on all a degree of supervision and security which is determined by the common denominator of the group response to conditions of limited freedom. The concentration of large numbers of men in institutions built to house only one-half or two-thirds of the number which they now accommodate, compels a higher degree of lock-step routine than would be required were facilities more nearly sufficient. Economic competition outside the institution has enforced idleness upon too large a proportion of these reformatories (a problem to which the Federal Government has recently addressed itself) with the result that work, which should be the backbone and mainstay of the reformatory method, is too often drawn off into routine duties connected with maintenance and cleaning of the institution. Inactivity rather than industry is the rule in the majority of our reform institutions, with the inevitable result that good work habits, lack of which was among the factors resulting in the commitment of these young offenders, are not established at the institution to which they have been sent to be "reformed."

The overcrowding of the institution, the mixed nature of the groups committed there for training, the lack of facilities or of adequate personnel, and the requirements of custodial care in the handling of large numbers of men have resulted in a paucity of active programs to take up the non-working hours of most reformatory inmates. Some institution reports point proudly to the large percentage of their men who are engaged in sports, crafts, education classes, and other hobbies and interests. With very rare exceptions, however, institutions for the reform of male offenders do not offer opportunity for all their inmates to engage in some kind of after-work activity.

In appearance, and particularly in personnel, there is little if anything to distinguish the reformatory from the prison. Similarities in the qualifications, civil service status, remuneration, and duties of the officers in these two types of institutions are much more noticeable than any differences between them. Uniformed guards are an inevitable concomitant of a reformatory system which differs only in name from the more severe type of prison which it was intended to supplant—and which it too often only emulates. The experience and qualifications of the men who staff these reformatories would not fit them for the task of influencing for the better the habits and attitudes of inmates, even if the surroundings were less unfavorable than they are. Uniforms, pistols, and truncheons, searchlights and machine guns emplaced upon the walls, the prevalence of a military manner, if not a military routine, which is inescapable in a congregate institution where there is no serious attempt to cull out the more reformable elements, all these things militate against a reformative achievement for which such high hopes were held sixty or seventy years ago.

And here properly may be mentioned another serious matter which contributes to the total result—the conditions to which youthful offenders are subjected in very many places during the period between arrest and conviction. Anyone acquainted with the facts can see every reason to believe that these conditions have a hardening influence. Judging from what one learns through individual cases, it seems highly probable that the treatment in detention prisons pending trial is one important reason why the human material in our reformatories appears so tough and cynical. Even if vastly better methods of institutional treatment are established, it may well continue to be difficult to influence offenders if previous to commitment to the institution they have been handled with so little understanding of human psychology.

It is hardly necessary here to dwell on these ineptitudes of police and detention procedures—they are forcefully described in *Youth in the Toils,* a study of boys being held for trial or sentence in the Tombs Prison, New York City.[1] The findings of the investigators, Harrison and Grant, were a great stimulus to the committee of the American Law Institute, referred to earlier, in the tentative formulation of a model Youth Court Act which would apply particularly to metropolitan areas. Our preconviction handling of the youthful offender is in marked contrast to the English procedure as set forth in Chapter VI. It should be obvious that the better methods of investigation and detention in England must tend to produce on the part of the offender a more favorable response to prescribed treatment.

Reformatory superintendents and state commissioners of correction publish statements of the effects of reformatory methods which describe successes in terms of two-thirds or three-quarters of their annual graduates. The Gluecks' study has conclusively proved that so far as one of our well-known reformatories is concerned, the rate of recidivism among its graduates is rather the reverse of that so frequently claimed. A full decade has elapsed since the publication of this important finding. That period has seen little real improvement in reformatory conditions the country over. It may be well, therefore, to review the conditions which prevailed in this institution, the Reformatory for Men at West Concord, Massachusetts, prior to the release of these 510 young men about four-fifths (78 per cent) of whom committed new offenses.

The population at this institution was not limited to

1. By Leonard V. Harrison and Pryor McNeill Grant, 1938.

the youth group. Of the 506 men whose ages were known, only three-fifths were under 21, one-third were 21 to 27, and 6 per cent were between 28 and 36 years old. (As a result of the transfer to Concord in recent years of older men from the Massachusetts State Prison, the average age is now higher than these figures show.) Nor were these men predominantly first offenders: "Over four-fifths of the Reformatory inmates are known to have been arrested for offenses other than, and prior to, those for which they were sentenced to the Reformatory."[2] Conviction resulted in sentences in 1,451 previous cases in which this group of young men were involved; commitments to penal or correctional institutions followed 42 per cent of these sentences.

Within the institution itself, the regime to which they were subjected kept them in their cells for an average of one-half of each twenty-four hours, ten hours at night and two hours during the day. Each man received an average of eight hours a week of physical exercise, if such activity as walking around in a closed yard is included as "exercise." Ninety per cent of the men worked within the walls which encircled the institution; the remaining tenth were allowed to work at the reformatory farm only if they had very short terms to serve or when release was three months or less away—provided their institutional record had been good. As for the prospect of any personal interest in or influence upon the young offender commensurate with his need, it is stated that "to spend an hour or less with an individual in the dis-

2. *Five Hundred Criminal Careers*, Sheldon and Eleanor T. Glueck, 1930, p. 147.

cussion of such need and then to leave him to his thoughts and devices for the remainder of his stay at the Reformatory will ordinarily not affect the life-current of the prisoner."[3] When the time for release had arrived, 95 per cent of the men who were paroled had jobs waiting for them, of which 12 per cent had been found by the parole agents. "Fifty-nine per cent of the parolees held their first job not at all or for periods of one month or less,"[4] which suggests that many of the jobs were in the nature of temporary expedients to secure a release. Most important of all, in over one-half of the cases (53 per cent), "the parolee himself was not once personally visited in the entire parole period."[5]

Recent reports[6] on the operation of the reformatory at Elmira, once the hope of progressive penologists, show how far removed is principle from application. The age group at this reformatory is from sixteen to thirty. Almost a full fourth, 421 (24 per cent), of the 1,703 inmates present in the institution on June 18, 1938, were returned parole violators. Because of overcrowding, more than one-half, 958, were doubled up in cells originally designed for one inmate. Classification is a cardinal feature of the institution: "All incoming inmates received from the courts are housed in C block for about one month during which period they are intensively studied in the classification clinic after which assignments to various activities are made." But the pres-

---

3. *Ibid.*, p. 45.   4. *Ibid.*, p. 178.
5. *Ibid.*, p. 171.
6. Inspection Reports of the State Commission of Correction, New York: May, 1937; June, 1938; November, 1939.

ence of the older offenders and of parole violators ("61 of these were returned twice, 15 three times, and 2 four times") largely negates the results of these excellent attempts at segregation. Separate sections are provided for the care of psychopaths, parole violators, and those undergoing detention for disciplinary reasons. In the words of the inspection report, "So far as possible, real first offenders, that is, inmates who have never previously been arrested for any offense are housed apart from others. However, it is not possible to continue this segregation throughout the entire institutional program as these inmates must attend educational classes and work with others."

The entire inmate population participates in a forty-minute daily drill in military training, as well as "in some activity in either the gymnasium or auditorium for two one-half hour periods each week." Other recreational activities, however, particularly in the evenings "are a special reward for application, co-operation and achievement and a boy must earn the privilege of attending them." The inspection report states, "The entire population is kept occupied from the time they arise in the morning until they retire in the evening," yet only two-fifths (641 or 38 per cent) are enrolled in evening activities; all others are locked in at 6:30 p.m. and "may read or listen to radio programs in their cells until 10:30 p.m. when taps are sounded." In other words, well over one-half of the total institution population spend an average of twelve hours a day in their cells. Evidently much remains to be done before this program can be described as one that "is basically educational and is so arranged that there is little idle time for the inmates."

Disciplinary cases, those inmates who violate institutional rules, are reported and locked in a detention cell "until the disciplinary officer has an opportunity to interview them, which generally is within twenty-four hours." In a large congregate institution housing half again as many men as it was originally designed to hold, it is not surprising that more immediate attention cannot be given to those who commit infractions of rules. The institution staff roster does not include, with the possible exception of chaplains, any officers whose work in the field of constructive personal influence parallels the duties of the disciplinary officer in controlling troublesome individuals—largely a negative task. Under such circumstances, it is not surprising to find that the only persons singled out for interviews were those who failed to abide by institution regulations.

A new approach is heralded in the Inspection Report of November, 1939. After the superintendent had been assaulted by two inmates in an attempted escape, "a new method of treatment is said to have been instituted with the highest degree of cooperation from all the officers. Under this plan the guards, teachers and instructors study and observe all the inmates coming under their guidance individually with a view to discovery of any maladjustment and immediate action is taken to correct any such condition. When an inmate is thought not to be making satisfactory or normal adjustments the teacher or officer talks with him, studies him and makes a report to the acting superintendent who makes a further study and takes such action as he may deem necessary for the welfare of the inmate and the institution as well. By this approach inmates are given special attention before they deteriorate too much and the basic causes are corrected if possible. In addition, several officers have been assigned to guidance work among the inmates in the shops and schools."

Certainly this procedure is to be commended. Incipient disciplinary cases are now to be treated before they become a real threat to the smooth functioning of the institution. The administration of reformatories is making progress if attention is being paid to individual cases of evident maladjustment even though that attention is in the interest, chiefly, of a well-ordered routine. It would seem but a step from the employment of these methods of observation and treatment of incipient disciplinary problems among certain groups within the institution to their extension to all the inmates of the reformatory. Confinement within the institution is sufficient evidence of the need for special treatment; it should not be necessary for an inmate to commit further offenses in order to be brought to the attention of treatment personnel.

In this regard, the institution at Annandale, New Jersey, which one of us recently visited for the purposes of this study, is particularly deserving of notice. This reformatory deals with a group of offenders between sixteen and twenty-six years, with a median age of nineteen. The population is not large—an average of about 450 inmates. The division of the institution into eight cottages, accommodating from fifty to seventy men each, provides an opportunity for classification and for something other than mass handling. Situated in open country, the institution is without walls or enclosing fences.

The Division of Classification and Education in the State Department of Institutions and Agencies decides, on the basis of study and investigation, whether an offender is better suited for treatment at Annandale Farms or at the walled reformatory at Rahway which accommodates men between the ages of seventeen and thirty. Cases committed to either of these institutions may be transferred to the other, by order of the Commissioner of Institutions and Agencies.

New arrivals at Annandale are placed in a segregation cottage for the first month. Here they are interviewed by the deputy superintendent, the disciplinarian, the psychiatrist, and the psychologist, and receive an introduction to the institution by means of an "orientation course" which is given by staff members. Few privileges are allowed at the reception cottage and a fairly full program is provided in order to build up physical health and to accustom the new arrival to the demands of institutional life. The next six weeks are spent in a cottage where more privileges are extended; success here is followed by six weeks in a third adjustment cottage where almost complete participation in the life of the institution is permitted. Four hours of school daily is compulsory for twelve weeks after reception.

After the first four months, allocation is made to one of four other cottages on the basis of the following classification. "Cottage 9" is reserved for real first offenders, that is, those who have no earlier court records.

"Cottage 10" takes those offenders who have not previously been in an institution and have had no conviction for a serious offense, although some may have been in court one or more times previously. "Cottage 8" receives those boys who have been in a juvenile or other training institution. Other groups are kept apart from the parole violators as much as possible; the latter live in a separate cottage and do not mix with the others except under supervision in their school and club activities or in their work parties.

An "Honor Cottage" is reserved for those boys who receive a unanimous vote by the institution classification committee as worthy of trust and a minimum of supervision. They are selected from the entire list of those who will be discharged four months later. Special privileges are granted, such as listening to any radio program they may choose, having a light supper before bed-time, leaving the outer door of the cottage unlocked (except between the hours of 9:30 p.m. and 6:00 a.m.), allowing their room doors to remain open day and night. During the night hours they are completely without any staff supervision: a cottage committee elected by the boys themselves maintains discipline, reports the number present, wakes them at rising time, and is in general charge of the group. In nine years there has not been a single escape reported from this cottage.

Each house in the institution is under the direction of a staff officer and his assistants, dressed in a regulation uniform, complete with Sam Browne belt, reminiscent of a state trooper's uniform. All other staff members are dressed in civilian clothing. None of the personnel carries arms or other weapons. The large floodlights which illuminate the central quadrangle at night are the only external signs that this is a correctional institution.

During the past three years, as a result of the interest of the progressive superintendent, a "counselor" grade has been created by the state civil service commission. The duties of a counselor, of whom the institution now has four (two full time and two who devote part of their day to other duties) are directed to an attempt to become well acquainted with as many of the inmates as possible and to help them in the solution of problems of a personal or family nature. They are on duty from four in the afternoon. They may take an individual aside for an interview, tutor him, or join in the games. They may hold interviews for an hour beyond the regular bed-time. From 10:30 until midnight they serve as custodial officers.

The psychologist describes his work as counseling of a definite type. He examines all boys on their arrival at the institution—his last word to them in these examinations is that he is at their call if they think he can be of service to them. Routine duties bar him from engaging in as much of this counseling work as he would like; it is seldom that he has an opportunity to initiate and carry through a definite course of interviews or plan of treatment.

The personnel at Annandale is selected under civil service procedure. The men are comparatively well paid and assured of tenure; they work under the direction of a professional staff in the central office in Trenton. These favorable conditions have had the effect of giving the staff here a professional status and interest. They are enabled to experiment with new techniques and to watch the results of their experiments. The spirit of the able and energetic superintendent seems to have communicated itself to inmates as well as staff, with the result that the institution does not reflect the sullen, grudgeful kind of atmosphere so frequently found in the larger, congregate, walled institution.

In this résumé, we have omitted any discussion of the really large reformatories where over a thousand men are held for training, sometimes two to a cell, behind high walls. The impossibility of working in any kind of an individual way with such huge unassorted criminal populations is self-evident. The brief consideration of an institution which has failed in the past to "reform" more than one-fifth of its men, the outline of a more hopeful regime now being introduced in the original reformatory in Elmira, and the review of some features of what is believed to be the nearest to a model institution in this country lead to the conclusion that there is much still to be done to bring our reformatories to anything like the effectiveness which the nature of the problem deserves and the protection of society demands.

PART TWO

THE BORSTAL SYSTEM

CHAPTER V

ORIGIN AND GROWTH OF THE
BORSTAL IDEA

THE Borstal System is the name given to the English method of dealing with youthful offenders, sixteen to twenty-three years of age. It is a highly individualized form of institutional training and treatment followed by a closely supervised period of parole. The statutory limit of Borstal control is four years.

The original impetus to the establishment of what has since become known as Borstal training[1] is found in the report of a Departmental Committee on Prisons appointed by the Home Secretary in 1894 to inquire into the administration of the English prisons. That Committee in 1895 reported, *inter alia:*

That an extremely large number of youths between the ages of sixteen and twenty-one passed through the prisons every year;

That, under the existing system, numbers of these young prisoners came out of prison in a condition "as bad or worse than that in which they went in";

That the age when the majority of habitual criminals was made lies between sixteen and twenty-one.

On the basis of these findings the Committee recommended that "the most determined effort should be made to lay hold of these incipient criminals and to pre-

---

1. "Borstal village stands on a hill above Rochester, looking on the River Medway, and gives its name to the prison for boys and to the system of training which is in use there."

vent them by strong restraint and rational treatment from recruiting the criminal class."

At this point it should be made clear that by decree of Parliament the control of all prisons and jails throughout the country centers in the Home Secretary. This control is the sole duty of the Prison Commission, which is one division of the Home Office, and the Borstal Institutions, with one Commissioner specially responsible for them, are under its charge. Another division of the Home Office supervises the work of probation officers everywhere in England and Wales, and the management of the training schools—the "approved schools"—for juvenile delinquents is the work of still another department. Scotland reserves to itself, though with much cooperation, a considerable amount of autonomy in these jurisdictional matters.

The fact that appointment to the bench is made through the Home Secretary—officially by the King—places the whole court-penal system very largely under the centralized direction of the Home Office. The entire process of criminal justice is thus seen to be vastly more integrated and close-knit than in our country where, under the highly departmentalized state systems, the various agencies and services—courts, probation, institutions, and parole boards—are discrete and function without the continuous supervision of a centralized authority.

In 1877 the prisons and jails of England and Wales had been taken out of the hands of local authorities and placed under the control of the Prison Commission. Sir Evelyn Ruggles-Brise had just entered upon his first year of service as Chairman of the Commission in 1895.

The report of the Departmental Committee referred to above enlisted his attention, and he determined at once to embark upon an experiment to prove the soundness of its recommendations.

The experiment began in a wing of Bedford Prison. Younger lads were segregated from the men, and "a special program of trade, instruction, drill and a scheme of rewards and encouragements to industry and good conduct" was introduced. The result of this undertaking moved the Prison Commission to state that "it is becoming every day more evident that it is by prevention alone, i.e., by concentrating attention and care on those who are young enough to be amenable to good influences, that this great problem can be satisfactorily handled."[2] A wing of the prison at Borstal (Rochester) was next set aside for the special handling of the new class of "juvenile adult" prisoners. By the end of 1902 the entire institution was devoted to an intensive program for this age group of "hard work, strict discipline, tempered by contrivances of reward, encouragement and hope." The principle of classification and allocation, which was to be an important feature of the system when it was more fully developed, began with the transfer of young men with sentences of twelve months or longer from prisons all over England to the prison at Borstal.[3]

2. *Report of the Prison Commissioners for the year ending March 31, 1901*, p. 14.

3. Throughout this and the succeeding chapters attention will be confined to male offenders. There has never been more than one Borstal institution for girls, now at Aylesbury, forty miles from London, with an average of only 150 in training.

Within the next five years, "modified Borstal training" for young prisoners was in effect in parts of the prisons at Dartmoor and at Lincoln. "The results achieved have been such as to justify a further step forward," reported the newly formed Borstal Association,[4] and following the passage of the Prevention of Crime Act in 1908, Borstal training was established in 1909 as a recognized part of the penal system. Power was given to the courts to order this special form of treatment— upon recommendations made in the individual case by or in behalf of the Prison Commissioners—for offenders between the ages of sixteen and twenty-one, the period of detention to be limited to three years in a reformatory to be known as a Borstal Institution.

Further experiments with special programs in wings of various prisons proved the necessity of separating the younger offenders from the older men, a principle now believed imperative in the institutional treatment of this age group. In 1910, Borstal training was discontinued in all wings of prisons, except for the women's prison at Aylesbury, and an institution at Feltham, formerly a county industrial school, was taken over. The Commissioners now had two institutions—at Borstal (Rochester) and at Feltham—devoted to a specialized program for young men in the specific age group sixteen to twenty-one.

Of course, from the beginning it was necessary to have a place of maximum security to which could be sent those few who proved too incorrigible for training under the Borstal regime. They and parole "revokees"

4. *Report of the Borstal Association, 1909*, p. 8.

were and still continue to be sent to a special wing of
Wandsworth Prison. An account of the place and the
procedure there is given later.

It was realized at the outset that institutional training
was only one part of the treatment process and that attention should be paid to the aftercare of those released
into the community. Accordingly, an organization known
as the Borstal Association was formed in 1904 under
private sponsorship to provide the necessary parole oversight (see Chapter XIV). This Association has, from
the beginning, been subsidized by the Home Office to
the extent of ninety per cent of its budget.

The Home Secretary, introducing the Criminal Justice Administration Bill in the House of Commons in
1914, said, "We do not intend the Borstal Institutions
to be anything like a prison, and as we develop in the
management of the Borstal Institutions, I can assure the
House that they will be more and more removed from
anything in the nature of a prison, and become more and
more purely reformative and training institutions." The
war cut short the development of the scheme; in 1916,
for example, the institution at Feltham was utilized as a
camp for prisoners of war.

Out of their association during the war years emerged
the fine comradeship of four men,[5] one of them earlier
connected with the Borstal System, who were to give the
system much of the direction it has since taken. Rochester and Feltham were continued as Borstals, and the
old convict prison at Portland was taken over in August,

5. Alexander Paterson, R. L. Bradley, Henry Scott, W. W.
Llewellin.

1921. There were now three institutions, and a system of classification and allocation was introduced going far beyond the original plan of segregation from older offenders. The most promising cases were sent to the Borstal Institution at Rochester, the tougher, older youths to Portland, and the intermediate grade to Feltham. During this same period, the academic work at the Borstal Institutions was placed under the inspection of the Board of Education.

For the first fifteen years there was little to distinguish Borstals physically from the regular prisons. In 1923 important changes were made in external features. Uniformed guards were replaced by disciplinary officers in mufti[6] and a start was made in the development of the housemaster plan which is today one of the most distinctive contributions of Borstal. This "house plan" was frankly patterned after that of the preparatory schools and universities from which the early housemasters had come. Some difficulty was experienced at the outset in accustoming disciplinary officers and housemasters to work together. The older men had been trained in prison methods while the housemasters were to have nothing to do with discipline as such, but were to concentrate on the recreational and educational programs which were now started. They were to build up constructive personal relationships with individual boys

6. This was done gradually by first asking the officers at one institution to wear civilian clothing instead of their uniforms on weekends. When they saw that a change in dress brought no lessening of authority, it was easy to persuade them to abandon their uniforms permanently. Staffs at the other Borstals soon followed their example.

which is even now their most important duty. Between 1923 and 1930 the groundwork was laid for the training of sufficient men to serve in the new Borstal units which were being projected.

Starting in 1922, the important principle of diagnostic study for allocation was developed at Wandsworth.[7] Classification according to the individual's needs was even then considered one of the fundamentals of the Borstal System. Case studies were necessary for such classification in order to govern the allocation to the three institutions which then composed the Borstal System. The methods now used are described in a later chapter. It is sufficient here to note the early recognition of the need for study and classification, which were carried on in a special institution. To this institution were committed for a preliminary month of observation all those from sixteen to twenty-one who had been sentenced to Borstal training in any court in England and Wales.

Before long the increase in the number of commitments to Borstal necessitated the creation of additional facilities: "Among the many conditions of successful Borstal training, this stands out clearly, that the institutions must not be crowded. Individual attention is the key to the whole system. When the numbers become too large this can no longer be given; individuality is lost, and the place, however orderly, smart, clean and effi-

7. Later this place of observation or "collecting center" for lads sentenced to Borstal was removed to a special wing of the prison at Wormwood Scrubs, just outside London. In September, 1939, for the reasons given on page 169 it was transferred to Feltham.

cient it may appear to the visitor, has become mechanical."[8] For the first three units the Prison Commission had transferred old structures to the Borstal division and had made them over as best they could for the introduction of the more progressive training methods. The results of these remodelings were not in all ways what was desired.

In 1930 an entirely different type of institution was carefully planned. The boys and staff who were to start the new unit were specially selected from among the Feltham population, and for six months they lived and worked together in a separate house there in order to become acquainted and to set out as a unified group. A farm of five hundred acres was purchased in the small village of Lowdham near Nottingham. The staff with sixty boys marched one hundred and thirty-two miles to the new location. The first year was spent in terracing the hilly site and in the erection of huts which were to replace the tents in which they lived during the early months. Men and boys worked together in the hard physical toil required to level the ground and to prepare the foundations of the splendid buildings which were later to go up under the hands of the boys. The governor of this new experiment realized the importance of developing community support for the project, and made a special point of cultivating the interest of the villagers who were at first suspicious of the "young convicts," now become their near neighbors. Permission was

8. *Report of the Prison Commissioners for the year ending March 31, 1925*, p. 23.

received from the local education authority to allow the
boys to join in the classes given for young townspeople.

The Lowdham Grange venture proved the effectiveness of integrating the group who were to start a new
unit and demonstrated the response which may be expected from young men who can be appealed to by a
new and exciting venture. Despite economic and administrative pressure to make the institution large, the numbers admitted to Lowdham were kept low in order to
assure the successful adoption of new persons into the
circle of the original pioneers.

Meanwhile the need was demonstrated for a separate
institution for the younger "toughs" of the same type
as the difficult older youths sent to Portland. The prison
at Camp Hill in the Isle of Wight, formerly used for
men serving long terms, was taken over for this purpose
in 1931.

By this time the judges of the courts were becoming
convinced that Borstal was a more effective form of
treatment for youthful offenders than short terms in
jail or longer terms in prison. As a result, the number of
commitments to Borstals was rising and there was need
for still another institution. In 1932 another experiment
was tried in the Sherwood prison at Nottingham. It was
opened with thirty-five of the oldest, most hardened
type of offenders, many of them married, many of them
deserters from the various armed services.

The Borstal System, so far, had made a boy wait for
twelve months before special privileges, such as smok-
ing and pay, were granted him. The governor who had

been charged with the establishment of Sherwood believed it was paradoxical to expect that young men could
be trained by a system which was the reverse of what
obtained in the outside world. So full privileges were
given to each inmate from his very first day, and he was
not deprived of them unless he failed. Grades were not
earned as in the other Borstals. At Sherwood each man
was *automatically advanced* toward release every three
months. The end of the first twelve months would find
him in the equivalent of the discharge class in other
Borstals, but here discharge did not always follow as a
result of entrance into this class. A man might be detained in the "release" for two years after he had entered it. In such cases the reasons for his failure to be
paroled were explored jointly by the man and members
of the staff.

Side by side with this automatic granting of grade
progress, a highly individualized program of interviews
and conferences was developed. Detailed charts of progress were kept for each man. Conferences about him
took place at frequent intervals, and all the members of
the carefully selected staff of experienced officers were
acquainted with his problems and progress. This experiment proved the value of intensive individual work
even with the somewhat older offenders. As a result of
this Sherwood experience, the upper age limit for Borstal sentences was raised to twenty-three. A provision in
the original Prevention of Crime Act of 1908 permitted
the Home Secretary to raise by two years the original
maximum age of twenty-one when, in his discretion, this
change was warranted. A quarter of a century of experi-

ment, plus the results of the work at Sherwood, justified this age increase, which immensely broadened the scope and potential effectiveness of Borstal training.[9]

By 1934 the increase in the number of institutions justified the appointment of one Commissioner who was given responsibility for control of the Borstals. Since then the Prison Commission sits as a group only in regard to matters of general policy. Any one member may make a decision regarding a Borstal inmate without necessarily consulting the other members of the Commission, but the Commissioner for Borstal is responsible for general oversight of Borstal matters. This gives the needed continuity of personal attention and allows for the greater degree of coordination of the system which experimentation with new programs and individualization of treatment within the institution have made especially necessary.

North Sea Camp, which opened in May, 1935, is located on the seashore near Boston, Lincolnshire, on the edge of the best farming and truck gardening country of the East Coast. As with the beginnings of Lowdham Grange, the boys who were to be the pioneers were collected at one institution, where they spent two months in preparation for a trek across country. The aim of this institution was to offer a challenge to youths who were relatively mild offenders, in the expectation that the healthy outdoor life and the adventure involved in reclaiming the rich marsh land from the North Sea might provide some of the factors necessary for reformation. Here intensive personal work would be done with these

9. By an order of the Secretary, September 15, 1936.

young men, and the experimental nature of the Camp's establishment would be as much an incentive to the boys as to the staff. As an integral part of the project, close ties were made with the neighboring community life of Boston, an old city, rich in historic and artistic tradition.

This period of the expansion of the Borstal idea grew out of the body of principle and practice which had been slowly developing over the past years.

Men trained in the ranks as housemasters provided staffs for new experiments in reformatory method. In the spring of 1938, the eighth Borstal for boys was opened at Hollesley Bay, Suffolk, in a section noted for fruit growing. A tract of some fourteen hundred acres, which had formerly been a training center for unemployed young men, was purchased from the London County Council. This institution was to specialize in orchard and farm work for the training of boys from the rural sections who might profit from an intensive course of this kind. It was planned that classification according to individual needs should be continued within the institution, and to this end separate house colonies were to be built on locations scattered over the Hollesley tract.

The year 1939 saw the latest addition to the range of Borstal units, when the old prison at Usk, in Monmouthshire near the lovely hilly border of eastern Wales, was opened as the ninth institution. A farm of two hundred sixty acres at nearby Prescoed was acquired for a camp at the same time.

It was proposed to try a scheme of allocating here for training a small group of boys whose histories showed need for greater development of self-reliance and the ability to make their own way, who had perhaps fallen under the influence of older companions but who were essentially mild offenders. After three months of rather intensive discipline and training, in which emphasis was to be laid on physical development and hard work, the youths would be transferred to the camp. Here they were to live in tents or cabins and work at clearing and farming the camp property.

Thus we see in the present Borstal System the outgrowth of many years of study and experimentation. The early period was devoted to a trial of new principles of training and reformation in parts of abandoned prisons. While results were far from being completely satisfactory, they did prove the soundness of separate care of younger offenders. This led to the acquiring of several other walled institutions of the old type for Borstal use, until in the early twenties a start was made in those features which today distinguish the administration of these schools: civilian dress; the house plan; the separation of the institution personnel into disciplinary and treatment staffs; the classification of offenders according to their personality qualities, the severity of their offenses, and their educational and vocational needs. The thirties saw the building of new institutions and the introduction of a variety of treatment methods and of leaders.

During these same years there was a gradual increase in the proportion of offenders between sixteen and twenty-one years of age sentenced to Borstal training.

For example, in 1930 this sentence was given to 725 youthful offenders, while 1,872 were sent to jail or prison. In 1937 the Borstals received 875, and 1,275 went to the other types of penal institutions. Thus the increase within those years was from 27 per cent to 40 per cent. In considering this it must be remembered that in England short jail sentences are very frequently given for minor offenses.

The increase in Borstal sentences from 282 in 1909 to over 1,000 in 1938 reflects a growing belief among judges and the public generally that Borstal training is preferable to other forms of imprisonment for the older adolescent group. The Criminal Justice Bill of 1938–39 was expected to crystallize these advances and to map out further innovations in a system which had proven its superiority over a punitive method of prison restraint.

By the summer of 1939 the units under Borstal control with a total of 2,200 inmates were as follows:

OBSERVATION AND ALLOCATION CENTER FOR MALES

Borstal wing of Wormwood Scrubs Prison
(Later removed to Feltham)

TRAINING INSTITUTIONS

For Young Men

WALLED OR PARTIALLY ENCLOSED	ENTIRELY OPEN
Rochester	Lowdham Grange
Feltham	North Sea Camp
Portland	Hollesley Bay
Sherwood	Usk
Camp Hill	

For Young Women

Aylesbury

(A small institution housing considerably less than ten per cent of the total Borstal inmates. Since our study does not deal with girls, we do not discuss this Borstal further)

FOR PAROLE "REVOKEES" AND CERTAIN BORSTAL
TRANSFERS

Borstal wing of Boys' Prison at Wandsworth

When we visited some of these institutions after war was declared in 1939 it was clear that a structure and scheme that had been forty years in the making were being dissolved. Many of the staff members were frankly worried about their own future prospects, but these feelings were subordinated to a desire to allow us to see as much as we could while Borstal still flourished. (At the present writing many of the institutions have either been closed or transferred to other services.) However, from the standpoint of our investigative needs, there was a certain gain in the attitudes of these men. Remembering what the years of the previous war had done to their earlier efforts, they were anxious that as much as possible be salvaged from what was once and might not be again, in order that somewhere else, perhaps in the United States, their principles and practice might be reconstituted so that all that they had learned and done would not be forfeited. For these reasons at this time a certain objectivity was noticeable among the workers. The Borstal problems of the moment no longer commanding, their minds went back to what had been. An analytic and frankly appraising attitude seemed to fill the void created by the stoppage of immediate needs and future reckoning.

CHAPTER VI

COMMITMENT, OBSERVATION, ALLOCATION

NO one, even if convicted of an offense and within the present statutory age limits of sixteen to twenty-three years, can be committed for Borstal training by any court until the Prison Commissioners have approved his suitability for such training.

In the case of a youth between sixteen and twenty-one years of age, if a Court of Summary Jurisdiction, after making a finding of guilty, discovers that the offender has been previously convicted of a crime, or has previously been on probation and has broken the terms of his probation, and if the court is of the opinion "that by reason of the offender's criminal habits and tendencies or association with persons of bad character" he would profit from a period of Borstal training, he may be held for sentence to the Court of Quarter Sessions or Assize with such a recommendation from the lower court.[1]

In the case of a person between twenty-one and twenty-three, if the lower court is of the opinion that

1. There is one exception which does in unusual cases give power to the lower court to sentence to Borstal training. If a youth who has reached the age of sixteen years has previously been committed by a court to an "Approved School" (the equivalent of our correctional schools for juvenile delinquents) and has now been found guilty of serious misconduct either within the institution or outside, he may forthwith be sentenced to Borstal training for two years with one year on parole. If in the latter period he fails to live up to regulations, he may be recalled for one further year of detention.

the offense is of sufficient seriousness to warrant Borstal treatment, the offender may be sent to the upper court to stand trial. (For the given age group this parallels binding over for trial in an upper court after a preliminary hearing in the lower court, as we have the procedure in this country.)

The higher Court of Quarter Sessions or Assize can sentence to Borstal training anyone between the ages of sixteen and twenty-three who has been directly convicted by this court of an offense for which he could be sentenced to "penal servitude" or imprisonment, even though no proof of previous conviction or failure on probation is offered.

The Prison Commissioners are under a statutory obligation to report to the sentencing court as to the offender's ". . . suitability for treatment in a Borstal Institution, and (the court) shall be satisfied that the character, state of health and mental condition are such that the offender is likely to profit by such instructional discipline." The responsibility of the Commissioners for such a report extends to persons on bail as well as to those who are held on remand.

The sentencing court may and frequently does have at hand preliminary reports on the offender's physical and mental condition and on his general social behavior, as well as the specific report and recommendations of some Borstal authority who has been assigned to study the case. The preliminary report derives from investigations by probation officers and the police. We have seen some of these statements by the police which are excellent examples of case history writing, over and above inclusion of the entire data on offenses and convictions. Sometimes they have much to say about the offender's school and employment record as well as about his associates. Criminal histories and fingerprints are cleared through the Central Record Office at Scotland Yard. The police are required to state sources of information and whether the information has been verified. Of course, it is only in the exceptional case that the police report is at all as thorough as that of the Borstal investigation which naturally covers information from parents, schools, probation officers, police, institutions, and employers.

The latter data are gathered while the offender, if over seventeen, is held in a boys' wing of a prison, or if between sixteen and seventeen in a Remand Home—an official place of detention other than a prison. The older ones from the Greater London area are held at Wandsworth Prison. Those from other districts go to various other selected prisons.

The determination of suitability for Borstal training is based on physical fitness and mental ability (certified by a medical officer) and on verification of age; also, according to statutory requirement, the Prison Commission must be of the opinion that the offender possesses criminal tendencies or associates with persons of bad character. The latter provision, in accordance with the Prevention of Crime Act of 1908, is in order to satisfy the court that "criminal habit and tendency or association was proved."

Not only is the report of the Borstal study given to the judge before whom the lad appears, but the person who has drawn up the report, whether the lad was in prison, in a Remand Home, or out on bail, must be present to substantiate the report or to answer any further questions which the judge may care to ask.

The court is not compelled, of course, to accept the suggestion of the Prison Commissioners. If a term of Borstal training is not recommended and the judge nevertheless sentences to Borstal, the decision is accepted by the Borstal authorities. In the opposite situation, where Borstal is recommended and the judge nevertheless commits to jail or prison, the Home Secretary may prevail upon the judge to reverse his decision. While judges are under no compulsion to comply with recommendations of the Commissioners regarding commitment to Borstal, the fact that they are, as stated earlier, recognizably functioning as parts of the whole court-penal system tends to make them appreciative of what the Prison Commissioners and particularly the Borstal Institutions are trying to effect. It is important to note that the bench has come to believe increasingly in Borstal treatment for youthful offenders, as indicated by the steady increase in the number of commitments.

It should be noted that a jail or prison term is frequently preferred to a Borstal term by both the boys and their families, because the former is usually shorter, is not indeterminate, and does not carry a definite period of intensive parole oversight. "It is significant that many of these [the type of mature offender received at Portland] prefer prison, and apply to be transferred there when they find that the Borstal system demands something more positive and vital from them than mere attention to a list of prohibitions."[2]

When a Borstal commitment is given, the judge usually makes some such simple statement as the following: "I think the best thing to do with you is to send you to a Borstal Institution for training." An important word here is the simple article "*a*." The judge has no voice in deciding to which Borstal Institution the offender will be allocated, nor the length of time which he will be obliged to spend there. It should be noted that the whole basis of the commitment is that it is "the best thing to do" for the young person. There is no note of vengeance in such a decision, no semblance of a decree of punitive banishment.[3]

From the first words which start the term of training, emphasis is on the reform of the individual, with the choice of the best means and the precise institution left entirely to the group who direct and administer Borstal treatment—the Prison Commissioners.

No matter in what court in England or Wales commitment is made, the boy is first sent to the observation center at Wormwood Scrubs for a period of about a month. (This center was transferred to the Borstal Institution in Feltham in September, 1939.) Without exception, no sentenced young criminal is ever sent directly from the court to a Borstal Institution. He must

2. Report of Governor of Portland Borstal Institution, *Report of Prison Commissioners . . . 1928*, p. 39.

3. It should go without saying that an individual sentenced to Borstal detention has the same rights of appeal to the Court of Criminal Appeal as any other person dealt with by the sentencing court.

first be studied and observed, examined and interviewed, before he is allocated to the institution believed best suited to his needs and assets. The right of appeal is meanwhile carefully safeguarded. Every boy is informed by the governor, after commitment to Borstal, of his right of appeal and a card to that effect is hung in his cell.

A more detailed study than that submitted to the court is now made by the staff at the observation center. This study supplies the information which will determine the particular institution in which sentence shall be served. A copy of the findings goes to the receiving institution where it is studied by governor and housemaster and where it forms the basis for treatment.

At the observation center, located at Wormwood Scrubs since 1923, a special group of social workers, known as "lady visitors," has been in charge of case history investigations. In 1932 this work was put on a paid basis as far as the chief, deputy, and two special investigators are concerned, although there are still sixteen volunteer workers, most of them without professional training. This group of twenty women makes approximately one thousand reports a year. The time of these social workers is divided between interviews with the boys at the observation center and visits to homes and social agencies. They render a service in addition to the routine of investigation. They perform the necessary function of interpretation of the Borstal Institutions to the families of the young offenders who have been sentenced there. Said one, "We spend a lot of time assuring parents that we don't flog their boys day and night."

Parents are likely to feel more favorably inclined toward a reformative process which is explained to them by someone sympathetic to the parents' natural concern. Some of them maintain their personal interest in the case; for example, one keeps in touch with about one-half of the cases she investigates, visits them at the institutions, calls on their families at home, and continues to visit after the lads have been released.

This work is under the supervision of a Voluntary Committee which pays the largest part of the workers' salaries; the balance of the salary account and all expenses are paid by the Prison Commission. The social workers are not officially established under civil service. This relationship between voluntary and official service is a marked feature of the whole Borstal scheme. It is illustrated by the above and by the work of the Voluntary Committees at each Borstal Institution, and also by the organization of the Borstal Association which has charge of parole and after-care.

The medical officer gives the physical and psychological examinations. A group test is given to all boys awaiting allocation; if a grade below average results, an individual Stanford-Binet is given. It may be noted in passing that in recent years any lad requiring medical attention receives it before he is allocated, so that acute medical problems need not interfere with his first adjustments at an institution. The proximity of Wormwood Scrubs to London has provided an opportunity for consultation with specialists in case of any unusual difficulty.

One advantage of the extended observation at the observation center is that epileptics, psychotics, and the certifiably feebleminded are sent to appropriate institutions, thus sparing the Borstal Institutions the task of dealing with these plainly pathological types of offenders. The administration of many of our own reform and penal stations is handicapped by the presence of such individuals, which to some extent make it necessary to modify a regime which is planned for the mentally normal.

For the allocation conference the data mentioned above are combined with what has been learned during the month's observation of the lad, which includes interviews by the housemaster, chaplain, and governor. Allocation meetings are held at irregular intervals as these studies are completed and a sufficient number of cases are ready for consideration.

At the conference there are present the Prison Commissioner in charge of the Borstal Institutions, one or two other members of the Commission, the governor and the housemaster of the observation center, the head of the Borstal Association, and a governor from one of the open Borstals when cases for this type of training are to be considered. The latter has read the records in advance and interviewed the lads in order to form an independent judgment about them. The summarized case material is presented to the group, and each lad is brought in so that any member of the conference may question him about his educational and vocational background and interests and about any ideas that he wants to express concerning himself.

Only after the group has arrived at a tentative decision are the written recommendations of the governor or other members of the observation staff examined. The procedure of the board is very informal and no official vote is taken. In case of disagreement among members of the allocation board the decision of the chairman prevails. The number of cases to come before the board depends upon the conviction rate in the courts. At one meeting attended by one of the writers, eight cases were disposed of in an afternoon. It is said that the maximum number of allocations by the board in any one day was thirty.

The problem of allocation involves many considerations. Mainly there seems to be the necessity for differentiating between certain types of offenders—those who are the more hardened, those who have special vocational assets or needs, those who are duller mentally or have physical handicaps. Length of time required for training differs among offenders as widely as the type of training recommended. Occasionally where a lad has had previous institutional experience an open Borstal is prescribed in order to discover what results may be secured by conditions of greater freedom. The board is frankly experimental in many of its decisions: "If you believe a boy is likely for freedom the only way to find out is to try him at it."

Since transfer to institutions with stricter methods and close confinement is always possible for those cases which fail to respond to the more open type of institution, the allocating board can afford to take more risks in its first decisions. The attempt to classify on the basis of the individual's strengths and assets rather than merely on the basis of his liabilities is thus made practicable. Of course the necessity for restraint has an important bearing upon the decisions of the allocating board, but other considerations, such as a commanding interest on the part of the individual boy, may alter their decision—as in the case of a boy for whom, by reason of his long record, Portland seemed indicated and yet who, because of his love of farm life, particularly of animals, was sent instead to Hollesley Bay where he was later reported to be making an excellent adjustment.

The homogeneity of the inmate group at the various institutions is also considered. The likely effect of a new member upon the group and of the group upon him is a matter of concern. The personality of a particular governor and the special interests of a housemaster are additional factors which influence the board's decisions. When a group of two or more were involved in the same offense, the boys are interviewed separately, before allocation, to discover whether their relationship is of such a type as to merit separating them by sending them to different institutions.

The decision of the board is not communicated to the boy immediately; the chairman simply says to him, "The governor will let you know in due course where you are going." If the medical officer certifies that special medical care or psychiatric observation or treatment is advisable the lad may be detained at the observation center for a longer period before final allocation.

Boys who are tentatively assigned to one of the four open Borstals are afterwards met by a governor from one of these institutions and are told that they have a voice in accepting this decision. A lad who prefers an institution of medium or maximum security may have his allocation changed if he is unwilling to agree in advance to conform to the conditions of freedom. If, however, he accepts the board's decision that he go to an open institution, he is told that this type of training, without bars or locks, requires his cooperation. A pledge is then asked of him that he will "uphold the honor of the institution," the pledge implying that he will not attempt to escape.

The particular type of boy selected for training at each institution is described in the chapters on "walled" and "open" Borstals. It is enough to say here that facilities exist in the nine Borstal stations for offenders ranging from the more mature young criminal with many previous convictions and commitments, including desertion from the armed forces, to the younger or milder offender with special disciplinary and trade training needs.

As more institutions have been added to the Borstal System allocation has become more selective and the need to transfer those who do not conform from one institution to another has been lessened. In recent years no more than five per cent have been so transferred annually. The board nevertheless makes some errors in judgment regarding the adaptability of certain cases to a particular institution. Where a governor or a housemaster believes that a lad should be considered for transfer because he seems out of place at the institution, a new adjustment within the house is first attempted. If this does not succeed, the boy may be transferred to another house to try the effect of a new personality and a different group of companions. Where this fails, the Prison Commission is notified and one of the Commissioners interviews the boy at his next visit to the institution. Transfers cannot take place without an order from the Commission.

After allocation and before the lads leave for their assigned institution, the subject of release and after-care is taken up with them. They are led to see the whole process which lies before them—the institution training in which they are to participate and the after-care by the Association to which they are to be paroled upon release. The Director of the Borstal Association presents this to them. The interdependence of institutional training and parole oversight is explained for what it is—a continuing process from sentence to final discharge upon the expiration of parole. Thus, prior to their reception at the treatment institution, these young offenders are led to consider the day of release, its determination depending upon their reaction to the institutional regime, and the terms of their parole and ultimate discharge. Borstal is interpreted as being aimed at rehabilitation within the institution and under supervision in the community.

When the lad arrives at the training institution, the Borstal Association has already started to keep a record of his case against the day when he will be ready for release.

CHAPTER VII

GENERAL PRINCIPLES OF BORSTAL TRAINING

BORSTAL training is not merely a single period of institutional treatment—it consists of two indeterminate stages within a four-year period. Flexibility is a cardinal principle reflected in every feature and department of the system. It begins to operate from the very outset of a boy's training, prevails throughout his institutional life, and extends to the parole period. The several ways in which it is exemplified deserve detailed presentation.

The offender spends from six to thirty-six months in an institution and the unexpired remainder of the four-year term on parole or "license" to the Borstal Association. There is thus a real flexibility in the ratio between the time spent within the institution and on supervision in the community under parole oversight. It lies entirely within the authority of the Prison Commission, delegated, of course, to the staffs of the institutions, to decide whether a youth shall serve a minimum of six months, a maximum of three years, or any period of time between these two extremes, at a given institution. Selection of the particular institution in which the period of training is to be spent is entirely at the discretion of the Commission.

Experience has shown the advisability of treating offenders individually, as far as the length of their term is concerned. Admittedly, the most important single fact in the life of an inmate—to him—is the date of his release. Most institutional heads believe that young men can best be helped under a system that is completely indeterminate within the maximum three-year limit. In contrast, a very few hold that offenders can best be handled by informing them of the precise date of their release in order to encourage them to work toward that date. For example, at the Hollesley Bay institution the governor has been experimenting with a definite fifteen-month term. He is watching the results very carefully and recording the reactions of different types of offenders to the idea of a definite time period. The fixed term is explained to the lad when he is ready to leave the classification center, so that he will know what to expect. It is the belief of this governor that when a young man knows that he has a set time to serve, he will not attempt to play up to the staff because he knows that will not shorten his term. Bad conduct may extend the time spent at this institution, but perfect conduct cannot reduce it. It is said that this experiment with certain types of lads was having the very definite effect of reducing the amount of "crawling" which is one of the difficulties confronting any institutional administrator—an assumed subservience and outward conformity without any revelation of the inner life or the real springs of conduct, which may, in reality, be unaffected by the institution regime. The reduction of "crawling" makes possible a better knowledge of the offender, with the inevitable result that the staff are able to do more for him by way of changing his fundamental attitudes, no matter by what name the process is called or how it is effected. There is

the added factor that, under this limited short term, the
work of reformation must be done faster and more intensively, which necessitates experimentation with new
techniques and methods.

Borstal training started as an experimental procedure.
Its development has been the result of a continuous
process of trial and error. This attitude carries over from
the Commissioners to the governors of institutions and
to the housemasters in charge of smaller groups. There
is general realization that there is no one "best way" or
"only way" to handle young offenders.

The principle of flexibility holds good even in relation to selection of personnel: the Commission seeks out
a wide variety of the best possible personalities with different life experiences to serve as governors and staff
members of the institutions, and then turns them loose
to grapple with the problem. The offender is allocated
to the institution and to the man who may be expected to
have the greatest influence on him. Because of the small-
ness of each institutional unit, it is possible to maintain a
fair degree of homogeneity among those who constitute
the group. From the point of allocation, almost complete latitude is extended to governors and their staffs to
deal with these young men as they think best. Supervision by the Prison Commission gives necessary oversight
of the process, and annual conferences of Borstal personnel assure the sharing of experiences.

Even the matter of cost is variable. For example,
while the annual per capita cost of Borstal training averages approximately $715 at all the institutions, the ex-
pense of constructing and furnishing the various Borstal

units varies tremendously—from $30,000 for the prison and camp combination at Usk to $800,000 for the very complete and elaborate establishment at Lowdham Grange. Various ratios of staff to inmate group are also found. At Feltham there are approximately 3.4 boys to each member of the staff. This institution, like the other walled units, provides one housemaster or deputy house-master for every thirty-five to forty boys. At Usk and North Sea Camp there is a greater emphasis on individual work and here one housemaster or deputy is provided for every fifteen to twenty boys. At these open Borstals, the high ratio of housemasters to boys compensates for the small number of other officers.

Many plans for experiments in physical plant as well as in methods and programs have come out of conferences of governors and housemasters. The Home Office encourages the originating and application of new ideas. Within limits, the governor is allowed great latitude in the conduct of his institution, and he passes this same freedom on to his subordinates in their dealing with the inmate group. A "Standing Order Book" outlines the regulations under which Borstals, like prisons, are expected to operate. It is worth noting, however, that governors make a point of emphasizing the purely negative nature of these regulations. They look upon them as a guide to what may *not* be done. Beyond this they feel perfectly free, therefore, to determine for themselves what they may do. Several governors stressed to us the necessity for this kind of freedom in the operation of their institutions, and stated that without it they would not consent to accept the governorship of a Borstal Institution.

The outbreak of war in September, 1939, completely upset the projected plans for the latest Borstal, which was to have been a training camp for the teaching of special trade skills by means of intensive vocational courses. The pattern for this latest institution was found in the experience of the Ministry of Labour which had trained large numbers of unemployed young men by this method. The staff members in the institutions visited, as well as the parole officers and supervisors in the Borstal Association, were acquainted with this new project which had emerged from an annual Borstal staff conference. It was a frequent topic of conversation among them.

Through the give and take of discussion, the Commission keeps its workers informed of new developments and receives suggestions from them. Not only were early failures kept at a minimum by these means, but the staff was able to maintain a high point of interest in the development of the system. Where a premium is put on experimentation and originality, a service is more likely to attract a high type of personnel than where all is routine and established precedent. This is not to say that all features of Borstal training are constantly in a state of flux. It would be fairer to say that constant evaluation and criticism are expected, and new departures are frankly encouraged. Such evaluation marked the early days of Borstal development, even before it had been formally recognized by Act of Parliament: "A careful record of each case will be kept showing the effect of the special treatment and its results, and, as far as possible, the history of the case on discharge and after."[1]

Individualization is another cardinal principle of the Borstal process. There are two corollaries to this principle: initial study of the offender prior to any further disposition, and careful allocation to one of the training units on the basis of such study. Allocation to the particular institution which it is felt will best serve the needs of the young offender is a matter of deep concern. In these decisions Prison Commissioners, medical officers, institution governors, social workers, and housemasters all have a part. Allocation does not stop with the selection of a particular institution; within many of them, the governor selects the house, and the housemaster the group in which the needs and abilities of the lad will be most fully met.

The larger the number of available units, the more discriminating is the process of allocation. In the days when only one institution was available, age constituted the only basis for Borstal commitment in an effort to separate the youthful offenders from the older and presumably more hardened criminals. Three units allowed a classification by estimated response to different forms of restraint, training, and treatment. With nine units, it is possible to take a number of factors into consideration

1. Rule No. 13, Standing Orders for the Treatment of Juvenile-adult Convicts in Dartmoor Prison, *Report of the Prison Commissioners for the year ending March 31, 1907*, p. 122.

and to allocate on the basis of such differentiations as needs and potentialities of various kinds.

The job of allocation becomes more challenging with each new institution added to the system. "The increase in the number of institutions for lads has made it possible to allocate a particular type of lad to each institution and to modify the treatment as may be found most suitable to the type of lad located there. It has also made it possible to reduce the number of inmates in each institution so that each lad may receive more individual attention."[2] Every group contains a small proportion of erratic and unstable boys and it is up to the housemaster to discover the best way of handling them by experimenting, successively, with different approaches. He tries to discover their interests and emphasizes these, whether they be sports, trade training, special hobbies, or other activities. Centering on the things that have the greatest appeal for such boys has been found the best way to attain an influence over them.

The members of the various Borstal staffs were the first to point out a third principle, namely, the necessity for placing emphasis on the "intangibles" in their system as against too great an attention to buildings and equipment. The fact that the system was handicapped by starting in separate wings of adult prisons and has in part continued in outmoded and remodeled buildings shows that the success of a truly reformatory system must depend on those elements which are not measured by bricks and mortar nor estimated by the modernity of

2. *Report of the Prison Commissioners . . . 1934*, p. 7.

machinery. It should also be noted that while the highest success rates have been found in the newer units, this is because the more reformable types are sent there for training rather than because these units have any special advantage by reason of their physical equipment.

In an appraisal of these "intangible elements" none appears more important than personnel. "It is the declared policy of our Service in these times that we should first get hold of the best men possible, from whatever source they may be found, and then give them as wide a scope as possible."[3] The men who administer the system are as important in reformation as in any other process which directly affects human lives. Where young offenders are concerned, it is undeniable that little lasting improvement ever takes place without some strong personal influence. The importance of this element in the success of the Borstal System has been nowhere better stated than by the men who administer it. "Success or failure depends not upon scheme or plan, but upon the sincere desire of the individual to know the lad of whom he has charge; to give a generous measure of individual attention to his particular needs; and above all, to care *wholeheartedly* for the lad as he is."[4] "Lads have no use for virtue in the abstract, and they will love and follow virtue only when they see it exemplified in someone they admire and respect."[5]

3. *The Principles of the Borstal System*, Prison Commission, Home Office, 1932, p. 20.

4. Report of the Governor of Camp Hill Borstal Institution, *Report of the Prison Commissioners . . . 1937*, p. 55.

5. Report of the Governor of Feltham Borstal Institution, *ibid.*, p. 61.

Borstal Institutions are communities in a sense unknown in most of our reformatories. Unmarried housemasters often live in the same building as the boys. Married housemasters and disciplinary officers live in close proximity to the institution, frequently in houses on the institution grounds. While wives and children do not mingle in the ordinary daily routine of the institution, nevertheless their presence reflects something of the outside world and makes the institution appear more of a community than do most of our American reformatories. Tradespeople come and go freely, children play about the grounds, dogs follow their masters about the institution. Flowers, baby carriages, automobiles, all give a sense of living in a community which is by no means insulated from the activities and interests of normal life in town or country.

One of the principles of Borstal training finds expression in the placing of young offenders in a setting of socially interdependent relationships, and the deliberate direction of house or institution "public opinion" is recognized for its value in the reformative process. The more nearly the microcosm of the institution can be made to resemble the outer world, especially in the interrelationships between staff and inmates, the more likely is the benefit of institutional training to carry over into the larger society to which the young offender must return. How clearly the leaders have come to appreciate this important function of the training process is shown by the following statement by one of them: "All lads now make their way to shop on assembly without any marshalling by house officers, and each is himself responsible for getting to work in time." He frankly adds that there is food for thought in the recollection that in earlier years they "tried to teach lads punctuality without making it possible for them to be late!"[6]

Persons professionally engaged in the reformative process admit that one of their most baffling tasks is to deal with the offender who conforms within the institution in order to give the appearance of having reformed, and yet remains essentially the same person that he was before he was committed and will continue to be the same person when he is again released. Exemplary behavior is sometimes only exemplary institutional behavior, the character of which is rather implicit obedience than growth in initiative and self-reliance. The only way in which real changes of attitudes and outlook may be brought about is to get to know the individual so well that he will not be able to maintain his superficial defenses and will be forced to reveal, in time, his fundamental motivations. To penetrate the protective armor of one who has been antisocial for years, as most inmates of reformatories have been, requires not only a long period of continued oversight and observation but also leisure to talk with the boy, a deep interest in him, an ability to get through to his thoughts, phantasies, and feelings. These are the prerequisites for any attempt at modification of attitudes, the importance of which is well realized by the Borstal officials. They are aware that some young men would be more willing to conform outwardly if it were not for fear of appearing to

6. Report of the Governor of Rochester Borstal Institution, *Report of the Prison Commissioners . . . 1935*, p. 62.

be "crawlers" in the eyes of their fellows. It is a cardinal point among Borstal housemasters that they should give the inmates every opportunity to speak freely with the staff, and it will be noted in a later chapter how ingeniously these provisions have been made.

The Borstals have been patterned, as stated earlier, to some extent after the "public schools" and universities where a large proportion of their staffs were trained. This seems especially true of the larger walled institutions with their separate "houses." All have their own sport activities, and there are inter-house competitions. The officials point out, however, that the "public school" plan is not altogether suitable to Borstal; for example, it is impossible to expect a show of pride in being a "Borstal lad" comparable to the pride that attaches to being a "public school boy."

It may likewise be impossible to develop in a lad a sense of loyalty to a particular Borstal Institution. He has been separated from his fellows because he could not conduct himself as do the majority of his generation. But where the standard of comparison is not that of the outside but of the institutional world, it may be possible to inculcate loyalty to a particular section or house or to a particular master. Out of this may grow a group spirit that will make up in part for any shame due to segregation. In addition, by being selected to go to an open rather than to a walled institution, the lad receives some measure of status. So, even within a community made up of such temporary exiles, there can be instilled a feeling of worthwhileness, of some pride, which the congregate institution may never be able to develop because its only sense of distinction is the shameful one of being locked up away from the rest of the world.

Previous lack of discipline is one of the most serious handicaps of the young men who are committed to reformatories. It is this lack which tends at times to seem paramount, and for this reason so many of our reformatories are run on the same plan as are prisons, where few considerations other than discipline have any place in the institution program. It is in relation to this that another fundamental principle has prevailed since the earliest days of the Borstal System. Discipline is looked upon as only one factor in the reformative process. The inculcation of steady habits is accomplished by an arduous routine which designedly absorbs the energies and attention of the inmate group. The Borstal day is a fifteen-hour day—roughly one-half of the time being devoted to labor, and the other half to education, meals, organized recreation, and free time. It will be seen, when this program is discussed in greater detail, that there is little time for the self-absorption and the unwholesome phantasy life which prevails in institutions where men are locked in at five or six o'clock in the evening and not released from their cells until rising time the next morning.

For this reason, also, there is little complaint by Borstal staffs of the problem of homosexuality which is so annoying to the administration of the more rigidly run reformatory institution. Young men convicted of these offenses, or suspected of homosexual tendencies, are usually distributed throughout the institutions. The regime of rigorous work and training, with a variety of educational and avocational opportunities, is said to diminish the problem. In this connection, it is interesting to find that governors of closed Borstals have noted a greater prevalence of the problem than the governors of open Borstals which allow a freer type of association in dormitories, impossible in the older cell type of institution.

Great stress is laid upon the necessity for getting things done, for making headway and progress, whether at work, in sports, the carrying out of institution assignments, or the correction of individual difficulties. While different systems of grades and privileges are used at each institution, dependent on the type of inmate and the opinions of the governor, these systems and their variations are subordinated to the chief objective which is the doing of a job that will give satisfaction and a sense of accomplishment. One of the earlier difficulties in the lives of these young men springs from the fact that they have not stayed at a task long enough to learn its fundamentals and to reap the reward which comes from continuous application. The habit of steady work, a full day of labor, study, play, and sleep, a growing physical strength as well as a sense of improved relationships with one's colleagues and superiors—these are the tools for correcting the deficiencies and lacks which individual boys bring with them from the outside world.

CHAPTER VIII

PERSONNEL

SELECTION of personnel receives the most careful attention from the Prison Commissioners. They do not depend alone upon written examinations for applicants; they attempt to attract the widest diversity in the types of men to serve as governors and housemasters. Fully one-half of the men in this branch of the service are university trained, but graduation from college is not a prerequisite. The men in the Borstal service have come to it from a wide variety of life experiences: former members of the armed services, businessmen, educators, engineers, those who have roamed and traveled, skilled artisans, farmers. Emphasis is placed on breadth of experience, on maturity and a ripened point of view, on demonstrated ability to get on with people. Lack of university training, for example, has not been a bar to the advancement of a former artisan of wide experience, who, after demonstrating conspicuous fitness as a housemaster, has risen to be a deputy governor.

Men who have had experience in social work or clubs have a definite advantage, yet those without this history are not banned if they have other qualifications. In recent years, increasing reliance has been placed on training in social work and psychology. The earlier view still persists, however, and young men who have graduated from universities are advised to "knock about the world" for a year or two before they may be considered for the service. Attempt at political influence in appointments meets with short shrift. The following note appears at the foot of the application for the Borstal service: "Attempts to influence the Prison Commissioners' selection through Members of Parliament or other persons, unless they are in a position from personal knowledge to testify as to character or qualifications, will be regarded as indicating that the applicant himself does not consider his character and qualifications as sufficiently good to justify his appointment on his own merits, and may prejudice his chances of success."

Selections made by the Prison Commission are submitted to the Civil Service Commissioners for their acceptance. After a period of probation, a member of the Borstal service receives civil service status, entitling him to sick benefits, pension and retirement allowances, and so on. Thus there is complete economic security. Advancement, both in salary and position, is not based strictly on seniority. The Prison Commission reserves the right to modify its judgments regarding promotion in the light of considerations of merit. In both selection and advancement, the best principles of civil service are retained, while at the same time allowance is made for the individual exceptions and abilities without which civil service may become a mechanical process as full of faults, though of a different sort, as appointment and promotion on purely political grounds. For purposes of comparison, it may be of interest to note that salaries paid to housemasters range from an equivalent of $1,000 to a maximum of $1,800; annual salaries of Borstal governors start at $2,200 and may attain a maximum of $5,000. In addition the compensation includes living quarters, often for a family, and medical care, but not food.

It is interesting to note that the Prison Commission occasionally transfers a governor from a Borstal to a prison and vice versa, with the result that some prison governors come to their work with long years of experience with younger offenders. Four of the present Prison Commissioners have served in the ranks; two of them started as housemasters.

The position of the Borstal governor is equivalent to that of a reformatory superintendent or warden in this country. He is responsible for the establishment of the policy of his institution—of course within the framework of the general Borstal regulations—and the carrying out of that policy in the daily operation of his unit. While he does not generally have the power to choose his subordinates, he may request the transfer of certain staff members to or from his organization. A large part of his work is with individual boys, and besides that, through his previous experience as housemaster, he also serves as case consultant to his housemasters. The deputy governor has responsibility for certain departments of the institution and also directs a house. When the governor is away from the institution the deputy is in charge.

Within the Borstal Institutions there is a clear distinction between housemasters and disciplinary officers. The former are responsible for the educational, recreational, and personal features of the training system, have general oversight of and responsibility for their houses, and are supposed to give attention to individual boys, their histories, problems, and needs. They are not concerned with supervision of boys at meals or at work, or going to and from their various duties and activities. For this purpose officers, likewise in civilian dress and completely unarmed (even in the institutions for the most hardened Borstal inmates), are also appointed under civil service. They have the same rating and salary as prison officers in the prisons of England and Wales. They may be attached to a particular house or shop, or their ratings may call for duties as physical training directors or cooks.

Disciplinary officers cannot easily change their status and become housemasters, although approximately one-fifth of the most successful workers with boys within the institutions have been recruited from this group. Such officers who wish to become housemasters are first required to take a nine months' course under outstanding workers among the Borstal staff. After a period of probation they may be transferred officially to the rank of housemaster and are eligible for promotion to the higher positions to which this rank admits.

But even among those who long remain disciplinary officers there is a feeling for the importance of the work. One who had been at his institution for twenty years described to us his attitude toward his job. Most of the boys, he thinks, have never had a kind word, and he regards it as most important that he get to know them well. A large percentage of them he describes as "young colts." "You have to alternate between giving them their head and then pulling in easy. If you know a boy, there is always a way of handling him. No matter how hard-boiled they appear, each one of them has a spot through which he can be reached—an interest in rabbits, a desire to go to sea, concern for his mother. It's tact all the time." He never has any difficulty with lads who refuse labor and never makes the fuss over them that they expect. When lads refuse to work, this officer simply insists that they stand aside—don't sit—with their arms folded until they would rather do anything else, when he says to them, "Go on now, you can work." He regards his place in the institution as "interesting—great job this—always something doing—always something to look forward to—one of the best jobs a man can have. You can tell when you have made a dent on them, when they start coming to you and telling you their troubles."

Two other types of employees complete the institution personnel: trade instructors and matrons. Trade instructors are selected from civil service lists on the basis of their proficiency in a particular craft and their interest and ability in handling boys. These men, like the disciplinary staff, have a set quota of working hours in the week and are not expected to devote long hours to the intensive individual service which the housemasters render. In Borstals where a substantial amount of the work is production for government use, trade instructors are expected to be able to steer the necessary middle course between maintenance of production schedules and the inculcation of good habits of work, skill, and an understanding of related processes.

There is a matron for each of the houses in a Borstal Institution, and one or two for each of the newer camp or colony units. Matrons are selected for their ability to deal with boys and to create a homelike setting. Their chief responsibilities are in the homemaking aspects of the institution—cleanliness and repair of clothing, table-setting, decorations, and so on. Many of these women are highly educated; two at one institution visited were graduates of colleges—in these instances, the London School of Economics and Oxford. Some of them are cited as particularly helpful to the housemasters in understanding the boys; they have a place on the house councils at which decisions regarding the boys are made. Their influence was quite in evidence at some of the houses, where curtains looked freshly laundered, flowers appeared on tables, and the general cleanliness and neatness of the whole house reflected detailed and interested care.

Each institution has a chaplain assigned to it. He may either be on full-time or he may be the local parish vicar who is called in for services and occasional interviews with the boys. The larger institutions are more likely to have their own full-time men. The question of religious resources at the institution or nearby is taken into consideration in the original allocation of the boys: members of denominations other than Church of England are sometimes allocated to one institution. The same principle is followed in the provision of medical services. Only the largest institutions have full-time medical officers. In other institutions where the number of boys seldom exceeds two hundred, the services of a local physician are available.

One important feature of any training method is the

relationship between members of the staff. A high degree of personal influence of older leaders upon the younger men in the service is found throughout the Borstal System. The latter are encouraged to discuss methods among themselves, and they have a very wholesome attitude toward the governors, consulting with them, regarding them as final authority at the same time that they themselves develop initiative. It is through this relationship that the standards and ideals of the system are maintained and even improved. Discussion of the relationship between boys and men will be found in the next chapter. Here it may be of interest to consider what kind of men these are who are placed in charge of young criminals, in the role of governors and housemasters.

The brief sketches which follow are representative of only a very small fraction of the total number of three or four score men who serve as governors and housemasters in the Borstal System.

One of the governors had spent his early boyhood with his father in a missionary settlement among the criminal tribes of India. He lived there for thirteen years, until he was sent away to England to school and college. Trained as an educator and already embarked upon a teaching career, he was persuaded to enter the Borstal service.

Another governor had gone directly from service in the World War into club work with boys in Liverpool. His success in the management of several large club organizations led to his assuming the post of personnel director for a large national chain of hotels. There he was in charge of selecting the junior staff members and directing their training and recreational and educational programs. He became interested in Borstal, where he started as a housemaster. His son is now in line for an appointment as assistant housemaster.

A housemaster at one of the institutions has had an extraordinarily varied career. The son of a minister and essayist, he left "public school" to enter the army, where he saw service in India. After the war, he spent some years as an auto mechanic in England, and then emigrated to Australia and New Zealand. There for eight years his assorted occupations included prospecting, road and railroad construction, lumbering, laboring, retail store management, work on a rubber plantation. Upon his return to England he was attracted to the Borstal service where he has been for the past seven years.

A young man who has recently come into the service received his training at University College, London, and went into teaching. His progressive ideas clashed with those of his school principal over the question of corporal punishment and he resigned his position. With his wife he hiked to Northern England where the two took jobs as operatives in a tool factory. He purposely went on the dole for two months to see what living was like under those circumstances and shortly thereafter got a job as a sailor on a coastwise vessel. It was while he was serving here that his wife saw in the *Times* a notice inviting applications for the position of housemaster, for which he applied and was accepted.

Other men in the service have had very different backgrounds: they have been engineers, air pilots, settlement workers, businessmen, army officers, telephone linesmen, sailors, teachers. Individuality, imagination, breadth and variety of interests are made the basis for selection and appointment. These qualities were especially sought at a time when the Borstal System was first pioneering in new methods of control and training. Recent years have seen a greater emphasis on experience in education and related fields, and it was expected before the war altered the situation that more men would enter the service from schools of social work.

Once they have been selected and drawn into the work, these men are given an opportunity to tap and develop their special interests. Each has his own ideas of how training may best be effected. It is to be expected that some friction will result from such diversity, but the men are nevertheless encouraged to experiment and to discuss their differences. At annual meetings of housemasters and governors there is much free interchange of opinions and experiences. For example, during the discussion of the Criminal Justice Bill of 1938–39, governors and housemasters were asked to submit their ideas in order that the bill before its passage might embody the experience of these practical workers in the field.

The attitude of these men is that their jobs are careers. This is illustrated by the number of them who have been gathering material for special studies and reports on particular aspects of Borstal care. One deputy governor showed a huge mass of material he had collected for the writing of a book on "the ideal Borstal." A housemaster was compiling a glossary of distinctive Borstal slang. (At one institution, the discharge inter-

view between housemaster and boy is referred to as an
"elbow meeting." This expression arose from the habit
of one deputy governor who was observed by his boys
to loll back comfortably in his chair, or to lean forward
with his elbow on the desk when he commenced his interview with boys who were being considered for release. His boys soon came to know that the first position
meant they would be placed on the discharge list, the
second, that they would not. Failure to win discharge is
known among the boys as "getting the elbow.")

Another housemaster in charge of education had developed a new curriculum which would provide a more
progressive, individualized course of study. A governor
had begun an analysis of ten years' experience in the first
open Borstal, in order to learn what had been its effect
on the lives of boys who had gone out into the world.
The devotion of these men to their work is shown by the
fact that at least three had been in the service for upwards of thirty years; four men in the position of governor or commissioner had come up from the ranks during the past fifteen years. The Borstals have grown
rapidly in the past decade, during which time six of the
nine units have been organized. This has called for a
great expansion of staff. Men who have joined recently
seem to be motivated by the same high degree of interest as their older colleagues.

The housemaster is on duty from 9 a.m. to 1 p.m.
and from 6 p.m. to 10 p.m., on six days of the week. He
is supposed to have one day off in seven, one week-end
off in four, and six weeks off in a year. These optima are
seldom reached. A great deal of his work falls on Satur-

days and Sundays when there is no labor at the institution and many of the disciplinary staff, who work a straight eight-hour day, are not on duty. Attempts to estimate the time schedule of several housemasters at different institutions arrived at an average weekly minimum of sixty-one hours. Once a week each master is expected to make the rounds of his house just before dawn, and a monthly inspection at 2 or 3 a.m. is also required.

Because of the youthfulness of most of the housemasters—the majority are under thirty—a large proportion of them are still single. Of the nine governors, six are married. The requirements of rough, pioneering work determined the selection of bachelors to start the institutions at North Sea Camp, Lowdham Grange, and Usk. As these institutions become provided with more comforts, married men are transferred to them. The argument centering about the advantages of married versus single men has been long fought and still continues. In general it may be said that married men are chosen to deal with the older, harder type of young criminal, some of whom are themselves married. The cruder camp type of establishment is found to operate better when staff members become a part of the institution, live and work along with the boys and share in their hardships as well as in their recreation. Some governors, however, see the advisability of transferring men from this environment after a period of training and experience, because of its tendency to make them go stale.

The fact that these men live and work in such close association with boys is recognized as requiring some provision for a social life among themselves. Each housemaster has, in addition to his private office, a room or small suite to which he may repair at any time of the day. While single housemasters may eat with their boys, there is opportunity also for them to eat alone—either in a common mess to which a small group may contribute or in the officers' canteen and club which is found at each Borstal Institution. Married housemasters and governors who have houses within the institution grounds may get short intervals of relaxation at any time by simply going home, and yet remain near enough to be on call. At the officers' club, housemasters, governors, disciplinary officers, and other male members of the staff may gather at noon or night for drinks, smokes, light meals, discussion, or games. The mess is entirely self-supporting. There is usually one room where matrons or the wives of officers may have light refreshments, and at intervals the club is the scene of a staff dance attended by the women. These are very informal affairs at which the men themselves usually supply their own music and entertainment. These various measures for recreation and relaxation enliven the daily round and meet the social needs of the staff members who are absorbed in the wearing details of institutional affairs.

CHAPTER IX

STAFF-INMATE RELATIONSHIPS

THE emphasis placed on personnel in the Borstal training plan is naturally directed toward the goal of building up constructive relationships. The preceding chapter has indicated how carefully the men who are to do this job are selected, how much latitude they are given in the performance of their duties, and how much importance is placed on the influence they may exert on the lads. In this chapter the relationship which is built up between staff and inmates will be considered in greater detail.

Governors and housemasters realize that, above all, the personalities of their charges often require remolding, and that this calls for a conscious effort to "put themselves over" by means of their own personalities and standards. It is the responsibility of the governor and the housemasters to create the human setting in which the institution is to operate, and in which training is to take place. "There is no telepathy more sure and rapid than the perception of attitude."[1]

A young person committed for Borstal treatment has a large number of persons directly responsible for influencing him, to whom he may turn for help and guidance. In addition to the housemaster and his assistant, both concerned primarily with exerting personal influence, the governor and his deputy, the chaplain and

1. *The Principles of Borstal Training*, Prison Commission, Home Office, 1932, p. 64.

matron are all available for help. While operating staffs, disciplinary officers, and trade instructors are primarily engaged in certain specific tasks of maintenance and supervision or occupational training, they are also encouraged to become acquainted with boys as individuals, to observe them closely, and to help them overcome their difficulties.

The smaller the unit—whether it be the institution, the house, or a section within the house—the easier it is for the staff to become acquainted with individual boys as the first step in the process of working with them. Each man gets to know his own boys well enough to recognize when they are "off their stride." Housemasters are on the look-out to give assistance, partly because of the boy's own immediate need, partly because of the danger that others within the institution may become affected. The governor's constant concern is with these subtle relationships between staff and boys, and it is due to these efforts that riots and mutinies are unknown at the Borstals in contrast to what occurs in prisons for older offenders. It is recognized that mass uprisings against authority are the result of real or fancied grievances which are allowed to smoulder unnoticed until a group of inmates has become inflamed. Any trivial incident may then set off the accumulated resentment. At Borstal, such individual grievances are noted and met early and thus prevented from spreading from one boy to another.

Each housemaster has a private office inside his house, and he is available at definite times of the day to anyone who wishes to speak with him regarding any problem of an institutional or personal sort. In the larger walled Borstals, there is one housemaster or deputy housemaster to every forty boys, and as some part of the time of each is taken up with clerical and administrative duties he has relatively less time for personal contacts. In the smaller open institutions, there may be one housemaster for as few as fifteen or twenty boys, and he has therefore more time to devote to individual conferences and interviews. "Reliance should not merely be placed on the chance of weaknesses in the lad's moral background coming to view in the incidents of his daily life, but by talks and discussions he should be helped to form a philosophy of life which will stand the strain of later difficulties and temptations."[2]

In these smaller institutions, frequently the housemasters and sometimes the governor join in the physical toil of digging, construction, farm or orchard work, and share in sports, meals, and daily routine. This plan was first worked out at Lowdham Grange and developed to its highest point at North Sea Camp. Here in the beginning the staff went out every morning on the marsh with their boys, put in eight hours of hard work in all kinds of North Sea weather, and returned to clean up with the boys, to share their supper, and to lead them in the evening recreational and educational programs.

At Usk, the governor, while walking around on tour came on a group of six boys pushing a cart of heavy timber up a slope. For an hour he helped by putting his weight behind the cart until the summit was reached and

2. Report of the Governor of North Sea Camp, *Report of the Prison Commissioners . . . 1935,* p. 74.

the timber stacked. Neither surprise nor gratitude was shown; it was evidently taken for granted that members of the staff, even the superintendent, were interested in the completion of the construction work. When staff members join in with lads in this natural and free manner, it is understandable that these exhibitions of friendliness will strengthen the influence of the leaders. Housemasters emphasize the opportunity which such work-sharing gives them to become acquainted with their boys and to see through the defenses which so many have built up against just such acquaintance.

There are numerous opportunities for seeing and knowing individual boys; the routine, the close association, the variety of activities, the special responsibility of each housemaster for a particular part of the program in addition to his house duties, constantly bring staff and inmates together in a natural and informal manner. Questions and problems come up on the job, on the sport field. Many of these are dealt with on the spot. The demands of the immediate situation often provide a more normal setting for influencing attitudes and conduct than is possible in formal meetings or interviews by appointment.

There are, however, in addition, certain definite provisions for making the individual boy's acquaintance. During the first month after his reception at the institution, for example, there are five group meetings for new arrivals at which the governor discusses the problems of living within the institution and the similarities of these to situations in the outside world. At the end of the series of "governor's talks," the doctor has the group for discussions and practice in first aid, supplemented by conferences on sex hygiene. Religious matters are referred to the chaplain.

From the day of his arrival at the Borstal notes are added to the case history which comes with the boy from the classification center. The governor, chaplain, and doctor record their subsequent observations. Housemasters receive a copy of the case record of each boy when he is assigned to his house. One housemaster scans each record to ascertain, at the very outset, whether the boy will require a great deal of attention in order that some deep-seated difficulty may be understood or whether the routine individual treatment which all receive will be sufficient. Newcomers are received casually—there seems to be little attempt to do more at first than admit them to the institution and allow them to adjust to institutional life. Several housemasters emphasized that this casualness was intentional; they consider it best not to go into things too deeply at the beginning because the new arrival has been through a disturbing experience, has endured much questioning before his arrival, and was probably sufficiently upset at the thought of beginning a sentence to entitle him to some privacy and an opportunity to settle down.

Any boy may consult the governor on official matters, such as complaints, at noon of any day. He may also see the governor at night on any problem of a personal nature on which he may desire advice. At the evening session he may stay as long as he pleases and speak with complete freedom. In order to see the governor, application must be made through the housemaster, who may inquire the reason for this with the idea that he may be able to help, but he has no right to deny it. Any inmate who still feels aggrieved after the governor's decision may appeal to the Visiting Committee or a Prison Commissioner. As a last resort he may petition the Home Secretary.

Daily there is a conference between the housemasters and the governor. At its conclusion any housemaster who likes may stop for a few minutes' consultation with the governor. This is followed by a hearing on "Governor's Reports"—cases which have been referred to him by housemasters or disciplinary officers for difficulties occurring during the preceding day. The boys concerned line up outside the governor's office and are called in singly. The person who has made the complaint states the facts. The boy gives his side of the story, he is dismissed, and the housemaster is then asked for his opinion. No set order governs the procedure—the boy may then be seen privately by the governor or he may be left alone in the room to talk over the problem with the complaining officer.

In addition to these opportunities to see the governor on application—at noon or night—or on report, any boy may stop the governor on his daily tour of the institution. This gives the lad the freest possible access to the governor and enables him to bring up any matter which may be disturbing him. Some governors make a point on rounds of speaking to as many boys as possible in order that those who wish to approach may not feel conspicuous. Other governors are aware that stopping to visit a boy at work, in the shop, or on the farm may be, in a sense, a fillip to the boy's pride. They realize that boys distinguish between asking for help and being singled out for attention by the governor.

An example of the finesse with which a case may be handled is the following. One lad was seen by the governor in a morning session on a complaint of having refused labor—hoeing a row of weeds along a garden path. This had been his second refusal in two days. He was told that continued refusal meant being placed in the "penal class." He stubbornly maintained that he wanted to be placed in this class. The case was put over until noon, when the boy persisted in his refusal and demanded that he be placed in the lowest grade. (It is said that some lads ask to be placed in this grade at least once in their stay at the institution, in order to demonstrate that they can "take it.") The governor acceded and the boy was demoted. On tour late that afternoon, the governor saw the boy across the institution grounds hoeing weeds, the same job which he had refused for two days. The governor went out of his way to walk across the intervening field to speak to the boy, pointing out to him that there was no difference between this job and the job he had refused, with the exception of a limitation on privileges. The governor talked in a joking mood, the boy warmed up, seeming to drop his defiant attitude, and sheepishly asked to be reinstated with his regular group. The governor agreed that he would forget the foolishness of the past two days and simply countermand his noon order, so that there would be no official record of the demotion. This closed the incident.

In addition to the information gathered from the case

history of every boy in his house and the opportunities
presented by observation and interviews during the
course of the day, the housemaster also reads the outgoing and incoming mail of each of his boys. It is made
clear that this is done not for the purpose of censoring,
but rather in order to get a better idea of the boys, their
families, interests, and prospects.

The record of one boy noted that he was the third il-
legitimate child in as many generations, and described
him as "desperately determined" not to have anyone
take an interest in him or make anything of him except
the bastard that he knew himself to be. The boy corre-
sponded with no one outside the institution, which deprived his housemaster of an important source of information regarding him. To make up for this, the
housemaster devoted one hour every day to him; it took
eight months before the boy's attitude was noticeably
modified.

Once a year housemasters are given a few days on pay
to visit the office of the Borstal Association and to spend
some time with their old boys who are now settled in the
community. This is not in the nature of special parole
work and does not replace supervision by one of the parole agents; the aim is rather to show the men working
in the institution the end-result of their work, to keep
before them the basic purpose of their efforts—the adjustment of the boy in the community.

Despite wide differences in the personality, temperament, and character of staff members, there seems to be
common agreement that respect for the feelings of the
youths with whom they deal is of prime importance. At

a staff conference one morning, for example, the governor informed a housemaster that the mother of one of his boys had written to say that she would arrive that afternoon to visit her son to tell him of his father's death. It appeared that the housemaster through previous talks with the boy was familiar with his attitude toward both of his parents. The best procedure for informing the boy was discussed at length by the staff, and it was decided that it would be easiest for both mother and boy to have the chaplain, now acquainted with the family background, break the news.

There is no set way for handling reports of a disciplinary nature. One governor made a strict point, however, of postponing decisions in such cases from morning to afternoon or from one day to the next, in order to allow time for the boy to calm down. He realizes that some boys are stubborn and look for resistance in order to justify a recalcitrant attitude toward attempts to discipline. He is aware of the necessity in some cases of meeting such opposition with a show of greater force, and in other cases of waiting until temper has had an opportunity to cool.

At a walled institution which specializes in wood and metal working, the trade instructor appeared to be specially gifted with an ability to deal with boys. He cited the cases of two new arrivals. One, a rather timid and withdrawn lad, was being trained in the use of welding apparatus. During the first day that he was operating it alone, a harmless explosion occurred. The instructor, knowing that this was not unusual and that it was likely to happen on a job outside, took pains to spend the morning with the boy in order not only to teach him how to prevent its recurrence, but to give him confidence in himself and in his ability to control his tools. The other newcomer, an aggressive and explosive individual, sought on frequent mornings for someone on whom to vent his ill humor. The instructor decided to tell the lad that if anyone was to be "picked on," it was himself. When the day's work was to start he made a practice of looking in on this boy to see how he was feeling; "if he was spoiling for a fight, he got it."

At another institution, during physical training class on the open lawn one afternoon, a red-headed Irish lad was standing with folded arms while all the others in the class went through their exercises. During the entire forty-five-minute period, he participated only in the simplest, least strenuous motions. Not a word passed between him and the instructor, and there was no comment from the other members of the class. On the following day, at the same class, the same lad was seen hard at work with the others and, in some instances, outdoing them in speed or precision of performance. The physical training instructor, when spoken to later, said simply that the boy was a recent arrival, that his housemaster had talked with the instructor and suggested that the lad was hot-headed and should not, at least at the outset, be given opportunities which would allow him the satisfaction of displaying resistance.

The deputy governor of one of the smaller institutions of medium security, whose duties included the management of a house, initiated a method of having as many interviews as possible with his boys. He tells all new arrivals that they will be called in from time to time for consultation on their progress and that they may expect to spend anywhere from a few minutes to several hours in these interviews. This is done intentionally for those boys who might want to see him and yet might be unwilling to appear to their housemates as if they were currying favor. A lad who comes in on his own to see his housemaster may let the other boys infer that he was called in for an interview.

One governor believes that no rule should be made without its reasonableness being first explained. For example, while taking a walk over the sunny meadow land of the institution one Saturday afternoon, when the boys were allowed to engage in any activity that they pleased, he came on two boys stripped to the waist, sun-bathing in a corner of the field. He explained the reasons why the general regulations forbade such activity, described the effect of overexposure to the sun, and allowed one darker complexioned boy to remain shirtless, while his blonder companion was told to cover up. This same governor refuses to allow any member of the staff or any visitor to smoke in the presence of the boys, except at such times of the day as the boys themselves are also allowed to smoke.

Some members of the staff are, of course, more effective and more natural than others in their relationship with their boys. For example, at one conference where the governor was hearing the complaints of the preceding day, it was noted that boys standing before his desk held their hands tightly clenched, defensively, and stood quite taut while they were being questioned. The following day, when the deputy was in charge, a greater relaxation was evidenced, arms dangled freely, and the general stance indicated less tension and antagonism. Some housemasters showed a distinct flair for dealing with their boys—tones of voice, gestures, the whole feeling of the relationship between leader and boy were eloquent of trust and understanding. This attitude was not noted in all staff members, by any means, but of nine housemasters in one Borstal Institution, three were obviously extremely capable in this difficult work of adjustment. In talks with these three men, it was interesting to note that two of them stated that when special difficulties occurred with any member of their house, they made a point of rereading the case record in order to review the general development to date and to see if they could catch any clue which would point to the nature of the difficulty or some means of dealing with it. It is not necessary to point out here how representative this procedure is of the best scientific practice—that any specific behavior manifestations are the result of the individual's development to date and that emphasis upon the genesis of conduct tendencies opens the way to the understanding of such tendencies and to successful dealing with them. One of these housemasters particularly mentioned his conviction that he never had any right to become short-tempered with his boys, that they had a right to find their leader always enthusiastic about his job. This could not be accomplished if the leader took out his own dissatisfaction on those placed in his care. When the housemaster felt himself doing just this, he realized it was time for him to take a few days' leave.

The relationship of the housemaster to his boys is that of friend, adviser, umpire, and father confessor, all at the same time. Housemasters are made to feel that while they may run their houses according to their own ideas, they must also be aware of their responsibility for the spirit of the house and its loyalty to the institution. One housemaster stated that he found the best way to know his boys was through extra-institutional activities —on hikes and expeditions and at camp. He had discovered that when he joined in with his boys at swimming or in the gymnasium, they came to lose their awe of him and to develop a closer and more friendly relationship. Another housemaster felt it was a real help to be able to talk a boy's language when occasion required it, and to this end he was grateful for his previous experience as a worker at various occupations where he had picked up a generous vocabulary of slang.

One governor stressed the importance of having the disciplinary officers take some responsibility for guiding the boys as part of their general supervisory duties. To this end he has made opportunities for officer and boy to talk together whenever the former has lodged a complaint. He has found that allowing the two to have the quarrel out has helped to clear away misunderstanding in the mind of the boy, and at the same time the officer is made to feel that on duty his function is similar to that of housemaster—it is more than purely supervisory.

These are only some details of a regime which endeavors to develop in a correctional institution opportunities for a personal acquaintance with each boy and a plan for aiding him which is based on that acquaintance.

There are various members of the staff who are interested and ready to be called on when the boy needs or desires guidance. It is implicit in the spirit of each institution that the personal relationships which the staff members build up with the lads are part and parcel of their work. The English correctional institutions, by and large, do not give as much consideration to the rôle of the psychiatrist in the reformatory process as we do. Nevertheless, the few incidents noted here do show on the part of the staff from the governors down through trade instructors and disciplinary officers the realization that most of these boys have to be handled from what one might well call a mental hygiene point of view. Moreover it is recognized that there is no one best way to handle them; the staff is given great latitude in the formulation of various treatment schemes and is encouraged to experiment with new procedures.

For the individual with deep-set troubles, such as compulsions, obsessions, or hysterical symptoms, there is very little or no provision for professional psychotherapy. Yet what transpires through the day-by-day relationship between the staff and the ordinary run of inmates, although not designated as such, is really psychotherapy. Whether these personal relationships partake of the nature of "transference" or "identification," that is to say, whether a governor or housemaster develops into a friend with whom confidences are possible or becomes an ideal father figure, perhaps representing the kind of "hero" young men of this age are likely to admire, the term matters little; the effectiveness of the relationship is demonstrated by the results achieved.

CHAPTER X

THE TRAINING PROGRAM

THE manner in which a boy is met at a Borstal is considered a matter of real importance. Newcomers generally are greeted by the governor. His deputy or the chief disciplinary officer may assume this duty if he is not available, but most governors prefer to be on hand when new lads arrive. Property and records are checked and each newcomer is examined by the medical officer. The group is then taken to the office of the governor who describes the routine of the institution with its general program and details what is expected of them for advancement in the various classes and for release. Full opportunity is allowed for questions to be asked. Boys are then assigned to houses, their kit issued to them, and they begin at once their life with the group. (There is no reception wing or quarantine section for new boys because preliminary medical attention and general observation have already been given at the observation center.)

In some institutions great weight is attached to the right allocation of boys to houses. The governors believe that next to the initial observation and the allocation to a given institution best suited to the boy's problem, the most important thing is the selection of the house within the institution to which the boy will be assigned. The needs of the particular boy are considered in relation to the inmates of a house and the personality of the housemaster. In these institutions such discriminations are car-

ried to a very fine point—even to consideration of the
particular section of a house where the offender will best
adjust. Some believe in the principle of placing a lad
with those different from himself, for the stimulating
effect this may have on him.

Others do not believe in too careful an allocation to a
particular house or group within a house, relying on the
preliminary judgment to use a particular Borstal. These
institutions assign boys to houses by rote, expecting that
such random allocation will fairly distribute various mis-
fits and problems. In this way they also get a variety
within each house and bring about a diversified population with beneficial effects from the impact of different
types of boys upon one another. They argue that such a
random assignment makes for better interhouse competition and in general is more typical of the miscellany
existing in the outside world. Thus it is seen that there is
no strict rule. This is one of the ways in which institutional staffs are allowed to experiment with different
procedures according to their own ideas.

For the first month of his stay, a boy belongs to the
"reception class." He receives special instruction and attention from physician and chaplain, in addition to the
"Governor's Talks," mentioned above. Some institutions depend upon the members of this class to do the
cleaning and maintenance work about the plant. In this
way a fresh group has the responsibility each month for
doing the drudgery, thus obviating the necessity for assigning it to a definite "work detail."

One governor places great emphasis on seeing the lad
frequently when he is first received, when he may be

still smarting under his sentence. He believes that then he may be more amenable to personal influences, before he has mixed with those inmates who have already served part of their sentences. It is when the lad first arrives, this governor believes, that he most needs relief from absorption in his own troubles. Other governors take an opposite view; they make a point of not calling the lad out for individual attention until his first week is over, so that he may have had a chance to get over his initial shock and the strain of adjustment. During this week the governor and housemaster merely acquaint themselves with the boy's record and note his outstanding characteristics. It is obvious that whichever method is used, much thought is given to the human aspects of the situation from the moment the boy arrives.

Daily Routine

It has already been noted that the parents of many boys committed to Borstal training would have preferred a jail or prison sentence for their sons because of the longer, indeterminate Borstal term with the required parole supervision upon release. The boys themselves would prefer the shorter sentence on the same grounds and for the added reason that Borstal imposes an arduous course of training for a full day of fifteen hours.

Reformatories in this country generally lock up their inmate body when the day's work is done; they may have twelve to fourteen hours alone in their cells until they are released for the next morning's labor. The original purpose of solitary confinement was to provide time for the criminal to bethink himself of the error of his ways and so repent. This notion has been only partially discredited by recent penological thought and the practice has been by no means completely eradicated in our reformatories. Too many hours are spent in cells, partly out of deference to the vestigial remnants of the old philosophy of "penitence," partly because substitute programs tax the ingenuity of superintendents, the resources of the plant, the endowments of the staff, and the requisite conditions of maximum or near maximum security. The Borstal day is so planned that there is very little empty time and consequently the opportunities are few for indulgence in unwholesome introspection and phantasy. The inmates are not allowed to go to their cells or dormitories until they are ready for bed. The elimination of unoccupied periods also serves greatly in diminishing the chances for undesirable communications and practices. Even the free time is spent in the recreation rooms where various forms of supervised self-amusement are provided—music, radio, games, and so on.

In Borstal the chief task is not one of "uplift" in a moralistic sense. It is a method of intensive training coupled with an opportunity for personal acquaintance between boys and staff and the development of friendly and helpful relationships between them. The aim is so to train the boys sent to them that they will be able to withstand the environment to which they are to return. The more thoroughgoing the rehabilitative program within the institution, the greater the likelihood of their forming habits which will persist after release.

The following schedule of the fifteen-hour Borstal day varies slightly in the different institutions, but only as far as minor subdivisions of time between rising and bed-time are concerned.

5:40	reveille
6:20	washed, dressed, bed made
6:20–6:30	physical training—outside in summer, inside in winter (a swim may be substituted for physical training in summer)
7:30	breakfast over, mess tables and hall cleared and cleaned
7:30–7:50	free period—smoking allowed
8	at work
10–10:05	time out for smoke
12	return to house for wash and dinner
1	at work
3–3:05	time out for smoke
4:30	cease work in winter
5	cease work in summer
4:30 (or 5)–6	tea and free period
6–8	evening program of schooling, classes, hobbies, special gymnastics; or in summer supervised athletics, swimming instruction, etc.
8–8:30	free time, smoking allowed
8:30	supper
9	taps

The weekday is divided as follows: eight hours for work, two hours for schooling or athletics, one and one-half hours for house duties and physical training, two and one-half hours for meals (four meals daily, including tea), one hour's free time, nine hours for sleep. For its effect upon these young men the system depends on the steady day-in and day-out enforcement of this routine, with a change only at week-ends and holidays. Work in the shops and on the grounds and farms stops at noon on Saturdays. On that day the afternoon is devoted to sports and games, special gymnastics or, for some grades, freedom to walk about the grounds, to sunbathe, work at hobbies, read or visit other houses. Some of the open institutions which have established particularly good community relationships are able to extend a large measure of freedom on these afternoons. North Sea Camp, for example, allows its boys to take bicycle trips into town, to go boating or hiking, or to engage in field work in connection with the institution's historical and exploration club. Saturday night in all Borstals is featured by a film, a boxing exhibition, or other house and social affairs.

Sunday morning services are compulsory for all denominations, the boys being predominantly Church of England. The walled institutions have services by the staff chaplain or a minister from outside; the open institutions send their boys in a total group to the local churches. Sunday afternoon finds some kind of hike under way at all the institutions—"route marches" at the walled institutions and a freer, more rambling kind of expedition at the open ones. Sunday tea is a "high tea" followed by a concert or play, with speakers and musicians from the outside donating their services. Attendance at evening church is voluntary.

It is the content of these hours rather than the presence of a routine, the activities rather than the apportioning of time, which differentiates Borstal from more conventional reformatory programs. For example, their work schedules demand a rate of production which is commensurate with that of the outside world. The lad's entire working day is spent under the observation of men who are skilled, not only in their specialties but in noting the difficulties of individuals and in devising ways of influencing them. Each boy is geared to a program of adjustment which will earn him release when he is deemed ready for it. Ease of transfer between institutions and between units within institutions allows opportunities for experimentation with individual training programs. Above all there is recognition of the necessity of keeping these young men busy. There is little time for indulging in unhealthy phantasy when only one hour of the twenty-four is completely free and even that one hour has to be spent in the company of a supervised group and not alone in a cell, the walls of which preclude anything but self-concern.

The daily program is more intensive, more congregate in the walled institutions than in the open ones where boys may be working alone at farm or common labor. These open institutions are well aware of the degree of independence allowed their lads, but they realize, too, that the type of boy sent to them may benefit rather than deteriorate from the greater freedom permitted. Training in the use of freedom and opportunity to use spare time constructively is one of the most important tasks assumed by these open institutions. In none of the nine Borstals visited were boys seen standing idly around, except in their brief free period, or engaging in desultory, aimless tasks. The pace is definitely forced; the impression is inescapable that the authorities believe in a full day, a minimum of free time in intervals between sessions of intensive occupation, and sufficient hours for sleep.

Academic Training

"Instructors should remember that the object of education is not 'a dead level of mediocrity' but to carry the lads further in the subjects for which they show taste and capacity." So runs an introductory note to the syllabus for teachers at one of the Borstal Institutions. It sums up the emphasis which is placed on individual planning of the academic training for all committed for Borstal treatment.

The school attainment of the average Borstal boy on commitment approximates the eighth grade in American schools. Special attention is given to illiterates who make up a very small proportion of Borstal receptions; they are released from their work parties for a special class from eleven to twelve each morning, and their evening period from six to eight is devoted also to intensive training in reading and writing. Class I, composed of semi-illiterates, carries these elementary subjects forward. The next three classes add grammar, arithmetic, history, geography, and general knowledge. In the fourth class, problems are introduced which are related to the work of the various industrial skills taught in the shops.

Class V is no longer academic in approach or content. It presumes a knowledge of basic subjects, and therefore allows the instructor to branch out into more advanced work and subjects of a more general interest. Discussions take the place of drills and recitations—the elements of politics, ethics, economics, and history are studied and boys are encouraged to take correspondence courses.

Very few of the Borstal Institutions draw their instructors solely from the regular institutional staffs. Feltham, for duller boys, is an exception. Here the disciplinary officers and housemasters are responsible for all the teaching. Over-time is paid to the officers but not to the masters, who are chosen for their teaching ability as well as for their other qualities. In other places, where the Borstal Institution is considered a part of the community, many of the instructors come from nearby towns to lead classes. Some institutions also allow trusted boys to enroll for credits in the adult education classes in the town or village.

North Sea Camp has developed the most extensive educational program of any of the Borstals. Here every lad is given school acquirement tests, according to the result of which he enters one of five general grades. Beginners have classes five days a week from one to three in the afternoon, in addition to the two school hours in the evening. At the end of each three-month period, every boy is tested in all his subjects. If he does not get passing grades he spends his otherwise free Saturday afternoons for the next month on individual assignments and special coaching. One matron with previous experience in remedial tutoring is assigned to this work. North Sea Camp was making progress, up to the outbreak of the war, in introducing individual programs of instruction patterned generally after the Dalton Plan. The aim was complete flexibility in the planning of the course of instruction of each inmate so that he might begin each subject at the level of his own attainment and advance in the various subjects according to his interest and special ability.

North Sea Camp also specializes in training in the fundamental principles and skills in the arts. This course begins with the use of simple instruments—rule, square, compass, brush—and proceeds to the practice of freehand and mechanical drawing, simple architectural rules, the use of color. Next the application of these to architecture and painting is taken up. A boy could then branch out into pottery, carpentry, metal work, carving, weaving, or rug making. These handicrafts were in addition to the definite vocational courses in motor mechanics, cobbling, baking, book-keeping, and barbering. At Rochester the gift of a fine organ and the volunteer services of an organist from the town make possible musical training for those who have special aptitude.

Since in Borstals the average period of training is under two years, it is obviously impossible to give each boy an intensive grounding in essential subjects and at the same time advance him, by the time of release, very far above the level of his attainment on entrance. The school-leaving age is fourteen for a large proportion of British youth, and secondary-school opportunities are much more limited than for Americans. Borstal aims to "refresh" its boys in the elementary subjects and at the same time to extend their horizons by introducing them to subjects which might otherwise never be opened to them.

One Borstal governor, a former school official, stated his belief that most of the boys, who left school at age fourteen, were deprived of a chance to develop an appreciation for cultural subjects in which they were just beginning to evidence an interest. He believes that when these boys are received at Borstal, the institution should take advantage of the opportunity to present them with a varied and attractive program. Some of these programs have been outlined above and in other chapters. The universality of their application is well instanced by the fact that each institution has a selection of excellent reproductions of classic and modern paintings, the gift of one Borstal governor, constantly on exhibition. Each picture carries a brief descriptive note on the subject, the painter, and his period. The collection in each institution is changed at intervals and is in effect a circulating library of art masterpieces.

Trade Training

The trade training program given in the Borstal Institutions is particularly noteworthy because of its high standards, the use of modern methods and equipment, the variety of trades taught, and the enforcement of a full eight-hour working day for every Borstal lad. Trade instructors are selected on the basis of their ability to teach as well as for their proficiency in their particular craft. A small proportion of the inmate population is busied with maintenance and laboring work, but as explained elsewhere, these duties are usually reserved for new arrivals or for disciplinary cases.

The constant aim is to stimulate each boy to select a trade for which he is adapted and to pursue it until he has gained some proficiency in it. Vocational tests are now given in nearly all institutions by housemasters trained at the National Institute of Industrial Psychology. Some Borstals use the results of these tests more than do others, dependent upon the resources available for trade training. The first allocation to an institution takes into account the individual's vocational experiences and interests, and these, together with the results of later testing, determine the training program at the institution.

In a research conducted to estimate the value of the tests it has been reported[1] that in 69.5 per cent of 200 lads assigned on a basis of the test findings, "the recommendations had led to satisfactory results as compared with a figure of 45.6 percent in a control group." The latter had been "allocated to employment in the ordinary way. . . ."

An enumeration of the trades taught at the institutions will show the choice open to a boy who comes to Borstal for training. The building trades include concrete, tile, brick, stone, and foundation work, painting, plumbing, carpentry, floor-laying, sheet metal work, plastering, electric wiring, steam and gas fitting, paperhanging, and roofing. Institutions which are not engaged in new construction teach these trades either in the course of maintenance work or by a special project, such as the construction of a section of a model house, which may then be demolished.

Cooking and baking which are among the trades taught are important because of the demand for such

1. *A Borstal Experiment in Vocational Guidance*, H. M. Stationery Office, 1935.

workers at sea. Regular examinations are held at the
Borstal Institutions by national bodies chartered to issue
certificates of proficiency in these fields. Expert laundry
work is done at several institutions. The making of or-
thopedic shoes for inmates in need of them is a specialty
at another Borstal. Carpentry, cabinet-making, and forge
and machine shop work is the program most fully developed. Power machinery of the most modern type has
now been introduced into the woodworking and machine
shops of almost all the institutions. Boys are taught the
use of basic procedures and skills required for the production of wood and metal parts, as well as the assem-
bling of these parts into the finished product. Mill work
and the construction of furniture and metal products,
much of it according to government specifications, are
done for the Prison Commission as well as for the Army,
Navy, and Air Force. The elements of mechanical drawing are taught in connection with work in wood or metal.

In the more open institutions a great deal of attention
is paid to farming, horticulture, greenhouse management, and the care of live stock. Borstal Institutions are
proud of the large numbers of prize ribbons won by their
animals in competition with outside breeders. The great
bulk of the production of their farms is consumed where
it was grown or sent to other institutions under the control of the Prison Commission. One farm specializes in
growing seeds for the other Borstals. Only luxury articles such as flowers and tomatoes are sold on the open
market.

Otherwise there is no competition whatsoever between
Borstal labor and that of outside workers. This is one

reason why the Borstal Institutions have secured the co-operation of the trade unions. Boys who have reached the rating of "improvers" (a rating below that of apprentices) in a particular trade have no difficulty winning recognition at the same level when they are paroled.

The habits of industry inculcated and the excellence of the trade training partially explain why the paroling authority has little difficulty in finding places for Borstal graduates. The fact that made work is almost unknown; the fact that the institution, a government department, or the nation is to benefit from their efforts; that they are not "sweated" to undercut the outside market, all these considerations must have some effect on the quantity and quality of work turned out by Borstal boys in training.

Wage System

With the exception of those in the penal class, all Borstal lads are paid for their work. Though the pay is small, the wage system has proven to be a great incentive. Weekly rates vary from a few pennies to a maximum of two shillings, with output and skill the bases for the reckoning. Part of their earnings may be spent at the institution canteen for candy, tobacco (this is in addition to the regular weekly issue of cigarettes), matches, and so on. Profits from the canteen go to purchase such things as additional sport equipment for the use of the boys. At Lowdham Grange, boys clock in to and out from work exactly as they would do in a factory, and tardiness is punished by deductions from pay. Every boy must save a minimum of three shillings before he is re-

leased and deposits are made through the Post Office
Savings Bank.

Discipline

It is difficult to isolate the disciplinary element in any
institutional routine and consider it as a factor distinct
from the general regime. That young criminals are set
apart from society and required to conform to a daily
round which varies little for anyone is in itself a disciplinary process. Deprivation of liberty is a daily reminder of punishment. But Borstal does not interpret this
segregation as existing *for* punishment. There are some
among the population of each of the Borstals who will
give more trouble than others and for whom special
disciplinary measures will have to be taken. The likelihood of their not adjusting is, of course, reduced to a
minimum from the beginning by the care taken to allocate them to an institution where, on the basis of all that
is known about them, they should, *a priori*, find a high
level of staff interest, suitable companionship, and work.

For those who refuse labor, or persistently rebel, or
attempt to escape, special means of control must be held
in readiness. When these are invoked the boy is said to
be in the "penal class." Such placement carries with it
loss of all privileges, but seldom lasts longer than two
weeks. Boys are told when they arrive that such means
may be imposed as a last resort. There are cells for solitary confinement at all of the walled institutions; modified diets even down to a level of bread and water may
be imposed for limited periods; stone-breaking up to a
few years ago was the lot of the repeated offender

against institutional regulations; monotonous occupations, such as picking oakum, are disciplinary tasks sometimes utilized.

It is the setting in which these measures are employed
that is the important consideration. In a Borstal, a lad
never sees a uniformed officer, pistol, machine gun, or
truncheon. His officers wear informal civilian clothes;
he has every chance to escape from the bounds of the
open camp or over the wall of the more secure institution. There is not the provocation to rebel, to kick over
the traces, when surroundings are free of suggestions of
restraint and incarceration. There is instead a definite
responsibility placed upon the offender when he is sent
to an institution where he is expected rather than forced
to go through the day's routine; where the only bounds
he is not allowed to transgress are those of his desire not
to remain and serve his term. The governor of one of
the Borstal colonies describes the unnatural restraint of
his first group, which came from one of the walled institutions. They were loath at the start to leave the central
building and could not believe that the institution had
not a single wall or fence, that they might wander at
will over the whole of the colony's fourteen hundred
acres. "They were staggered by their freedom at first."

Another governor describes the temptation to formu-
late detailed regulations covering every aspect of institutional life, which would make his own job easier and
even give the institution an outward appearance of running more smoothly. He prefers, however, to lay down
a minimum of rules—punctuality, respect for the property of others, cleanliness—and to place upon the in-

mate group the responsibility for meeting situations not covered by this simple code. It is the creed of this Borstal that in the outside world men are expected to work and to manage themselves and their affairs with little supervision. Therefore, after an initial period of intensive and directed work, the boys are allowed to care for themselves in parties of eight or ten, without any officers to stand over them. Such a procedure would be impossible without a staff whose chief responsibility is to become personally acquainted with these boys, to win their confidence through informal, individual talks, to guide them in difficult situations, to aid them in their work, and, in general, to understand them and give them some understanding of themselves.

Great reliance is placed upon the effect of a "public opinion" built up in each house by boys and housemasters. The originating of this "public opinion" largely depends upon a factor already mentioned: that while it is impossible to give a lad a sense of pride because of his sentence to Borstal, he may be encouraged by his selection for an open instead of a closed institution, and he may come to derive great satisfaction from being a member of a house led by a master of commanding personality. There is no reason to doubt that group spirit and group pressure, if carefully cultivated and directed in a reformative setting, can be as constructive as it can be deteriorative in a neighborhood gang.

The walled institutions for the tougher and more serious offenders have a higher proportion of disciplinary officers, while their ratio of housemasters to boys is only about one to forty. In the freer colonies the proportion of housemasters is larger; it may be one to twenty or even fifteen boys. These open institutions have therefore found themselves able to dispense with the system of "leaders," or inmate monitors, having an unofficial responsibility for units within the house. The older institutions have grown up under this monitor system; the newer Borstals have abandoned it because they recognize its inherent evils. The suspicion of favoritism and special privilege hangs over a leader who, while of them, is nevertheless presumed to be "touched" by appointment from above. One of the walled institutions experimented by failing to reappoint leaders as their positions were vacated by release. All privileges for leaders were abandoned, yet it was found that after some confusion, certain boys came forward spontaneously and took charge, with no formal, open recognition from the staff but rather as a result of a natural leadership inherent in the boys themselves.

It is the opinion of one governor that in training a lad within the institution, it is vital that he should not "get away" with any infractions of regulations. At his Borstal a boy who, for example, breaks his crockery cup is required to drink out of a tin cup for the next fortnight—a reminder of the necessity for self-control. He believes that cause and effect (offense and punishment) should follow one another in the institutional world as they do in the outside world, but that severity is not necessarily and of itself so effective a deterrent as immediacy and certainty of discipline.

A "Summary of Punishments and Offenses" in Borstal Institutions during 1937 shows that out of a total of

3,093 boys in training during the course of the year, one received corporal punishment (nine strokes of the birch), 194 were placed on some kind of dietary restriction, and 65 were held in "close confinement."[2]

When certain activities in which all participate are made choices of the group instead of official compulsions, fewer rules are needed, more cooperative attitudes are developed and consequently the number of disciplinary offenses is reduced. A voice in affairs which are relatively insignificant may bring about a willing spirit. For example, one housemaster allows his boys to decide whether they wish to eat in the mess hall or out on the lawn during warm weather. Throughout the Borstal units one gets the impression that routine and activities are intended to stimulate all the inmate group to active participation, absorbing their energy and eliciting their interest. The close relationship with leaders creates a unity and good will that makes acceptable in the program of training much that would otherwise be felt to be so routinized or arduous that rebellions, evasions, and infractions might occur much more frequently than they do.

Grades and Privileges

The nine Borstal Institutions differ in their schemes of individual advancement and in their attitudes toward privileges, remission of time for good behavior, and the like. The average term of training at each institution is different from that at any other, which fact is taken into consideration when allocation is made. Except for the camps, institutions operate with a definite scheme of rat-

2. *Report of the Prison Commissioners . . . 1937*, p. 98.

ings—"browns," "blues," and "leavers." The general scheme was planned to allow one year for each grade, but it is well understood that it is possible to complete each in a briefer time. The brown and blue classes are distinguished from one another by the color of the jackets and shorts which all lads wear. The leavers are distinguished by a symbol worn on their blue jackets. The walled institutions average a longer term of training than the open institutions, and promotion from grade to grade and from brown to blue is purposely slower. It is possible, however, for a lad to gain promotion so rapidly that he can earn one year's remission of the three-year term.

There are certain privileges granted to the blue grade which encourage the lads to work toward this rank. Members of this group get a higher rate of pay, they may stay up a half-hour later at night, write and receive more letters, walk about the grounds with their friends on visiting day instead of remaining indoors under supervision. The leavers may on occasion be allowed to go out of bounds or even into town on week-end afternoons without a staff officer. If they have been found to be very trustworthy they may be permitted to make a short visit to their home.

The open institutions, which run on a less formal system of grades, rely on other distinctions. At Usk, for example, the difference between grades is represented by those living at the camp and those living at the old prison building. The first three months are spent in training at the institution, where the work consists of renovating and painting the old prison. Those who pass the probationary period are promoted to the camp, where they live an out-door life and engage in a variety of work and recreational activities. At North Sea Camp there are three grades—"beginners," "trainers," and "leavers," the first two taking approximately three months each to complete. Beginners receive special intensive routine and instruction in small groups. The "trainers" work in larger groups under supervision. After a lad has been at the camp for six months the institution staff discusses his readiness for discharge, and automatically every month thereafter until he is released "on license." The aim here is to develop self-reliance as rapidly as the boy can assume it, and when he has won advancement into the "leavers" grade, he is expected to work and study with a minimum of supervision, to go into town or on trips by himself, and in general is trusted as an ordinary person.

Escapes

Institutional authorities, no less than the general public, are concerned with the problem of runaways and escapes. In any reformatory system where minimum security methods are employed, and where emphasis is placed on increasing individual responsibility and training in the use of freedom, this problem must be carefully considered. Borstal strives to reduce the possibility of escape by careful allocation. The governor of one of the open units frankly expects that boys will make a try for freedom within the first few days of their stay, before they have started to settle down. He regards such an attempt as a natural reaction to unexpected liberty.

The record of a boy at one of the walled institutions clearly revealed the attitude of the authorities. This boy was described as "intractable" in the housemaster's early report of him—he frequently threatened to run away in his first few days and told everyone that he would not stay at the institution but would abscond and never be returned. It was decided to pay no attention to his boasts and to make no change in his work party which would bring him under close supervision. Within a week he had bolted and was picked up after two days. His housemaster had a long talk with him, explaining that his escape could have been prevented if the staff had so wished, but it had seemed best—for him, because he was so determined—to allow him to get away from the institution in order that he might prove to himself that his period of training could not be avoided. Discipline consisted in removing him from the work party for which he had expressed a preference to one which he thoroughly disliked, where he was kept for some weeks. Later, after special pleading by him, he was allowed to return to his former work where he settled down well and later was elected captain by the fellows of his house.

The governor of an open farm colony points out to new arrivals the freedom allowed, the possibilities of escape, and the inevitability of capture. He attempts to prove that running away is "stupid" because the open acres at this Borstal allow a boy to be by himself. He suggests to his lads that if they feel like getting away they should run to the farthest corner of the colony, but not beyond it, lest escape and capture earn nothing but transfer to a stricter regime and a loss of time.

The open institutions have no provisions for locking up runaways, whom they may transfer to one of the security institutions, if they desire. There they may be placed under strict discipline for a month or two. Institutions differ in their handling of such absconders—one Borstal governor places a great deal of emphasis on the pledges made by boys allocated to his institution, and he refuses to take back those who have absconded. Another governor brought four escaped lads into a Visiting Committee meeting, one by one, and allowed each to hear his case outlined by the governor with a plea for permission to have them remain. He describes this incident as giving him a hold over these four boys which he had been seeking to develop in other ways. At another Borstal, the one at which the governor recognizes the early urge to escape, the usual method of handling the returned runaway is to have him work for a period in close companionship with the head farmer.

With 3,093 boys in Borstal detention during the year 1937, there were 135 escapes and attempts to escape. The institutions differ in the proportion of boys who abscond. Hollesley Bay with an average of 140 inmates, reports 8 escapes or attempted escapes in sixteen months. North Sea Camp had 2 escapes within the first two months of its establishment. The following year and a half passed without a single escape. The Prison Commission Report for 1937, however, lists 2 "escapes and attempts to escape" from that camp. In the first six months of its operation the Borstal Institution at Usk had 4 single escapes and one instance of 4 lads escaping together. At Lowdham Grange in 1937 there were 27 escapes and attempts to escape; while the walled Borstal at Rochester reported 33 absconders. The four open institutions, which might be expected to show a higher escape rate than the walled institutions where a stricter degree of surveillance and security is maintained, show, in fact, a lower proportion. In this connection it is interesting to note the observation of the Rochester governor that there were practically never any runaways from the open playing fields or from the summer encampment. On the other hand, the walls of the institution, especially the old prison building which serves as a dormitory, seem to offer a challenge to escape. In illustration he cited the case of a recent absconder, a lad who had elaborately contrived a way of removing a lock from his door and then had escaped through a skylight far above. This was a rather hazardous adventure on the part of a boy who might any day have departed through the woods from the playing field.

Whereas the newspapers make much ado if there are escapes from a Borstal, the staff take the matter much more calmly because they know that those who run away will be returned by the police or will come back voluntarily. The latter is not at all unusual, even on the part of lads who have stayed away for some days.

CHAPTER XI

RELATIONSHIPS WITH HOME AND COMMUNITY

COMMITMENT for Borstal training by no means implies isolation; indeed, contacts with the outside world are considered essential parts of the program in order to develop the boy's ability to maintain himself successfully in the community, as well as inside the controlled environment of the institution. And since the Borstal term is not short it is deemed important in most cases to keep alive the ties between the boy and his family.

Home Relationships

As soon as a boy has been received at the observation center, a form letter is sent to his family, requesting information regarding his early history and development. The social worker next visits the home in order to meet the family and to supplement the routine information already received. The family is free to visit the receiving center at special times while the boy is under observation and before he is allocated to a particular Borstal Institution.

Another letter goes to his parents as soon as the boy is received at the Borstal. Though the form of these letters may vary, they are alike in using this opportunity to seek the cooperation of the family at the very outset of training. The letters sent from the open institutions are interestingly worded, for example: "Your son has been given the privilege of being sent to Lowdham Grange for his Borstal training. It is a privilege, because only lads who are considered trustworthy and reliable are chosen to share in the extra measure of freedom allowed at Lowdham Grange." The letter goes on to describe the institution routine in detail, and gives the name of the house and housemaster to whom the boy has been assigned. The parents are assured that the master "will always be glad to write and tell you how your son is getting on." Directions for reaching the institution are then detailed. The concluding paragraph is also interestingly phrased: "If your son settles down here, no key will be turned on him during the remainder of his Borstal training. I hope that you will do all you can to help him to use his freedom rightly. All those responsible for his training will do all they can, so that he may do well when he gets into the world again. The great majority of lads who come here take the chance that the training gives them and are successful in after-life. This is due not only to the training but also to the encouragement they receive from their home. With best wishes for your son's success. . . ."

The letter sent from Hollesley Bay is in much the same vein:—"Your son has arrived here to begin the training considered necessary, and the first thing that I want to ask is that we may have your help and cooperation in the training that is to be given. . . . His housemaster is ——, who will be glad to hear from you at any time if you have any suggestions that may help the lad here or when he is discharged . . . it is in his best interests that I would ask for all the help that you can give in the way of advice and encouragement."

Letters are the chief means of contact between the boy and his family for the balance of his stay at the institution. While regulations stipulate permission to write two letters a month, as boys progress they are allowed to write more frequently to their parents and acquaintances. All letters between inmates and the outside are read by the housemaster. On the several occasions when this process was witnessed, there was no attempt made by the housemaster to censor or delete any portions of letters. Factual data as well as expressions of attitude on the part of boys or parents are recorded by the housemaster in the case history. Only when a boy is placed in the "penal class" is the one-letter-a-fortnight rule invoked. Housemasters and matrons add to the bond between the boy and the outside world by corresponding with parents on matters relating to the boy's adjustment in the institution or to his discharge.

A visit to the institution by a parent or other close relative must be allowed to every boy once in sixty days, even though the visit may be limited to twenty minutes in cases where the influence of the visitor is considered harmful or the boy is undergoing discipline. This is in accord with the regulations established by the Prison Commission. This limitation is very infrequently imposed, however, and boys who are doing well may receive visits quite often. An official visiting permit from the institution, usually through the housemaster, is required. Except where a visit from home may upset the

boy and interfere with his progress, such contacts between him and his family are encouraged as a useful
means of attaining cooperation from parents, and of
keeping alive their interest in their son.

One case record described the instance of a boy who
had very evidently been overprotected prior to the commission of the offenses which brought him to the institution. A rigorous course of training was prescribed for
him which was upset by the too frequent and too solicitous visits of his mother, minister, and former school-
master. Here the standing regulation regarding visits
was invoked by the housemaster, and the family thus
kept at bay long enough to get the boy to stand on his
own feet. Another record contained the story of a lad
who had become estranged from his father and had
drifted to London where he was arrested for petty larcenies extending over a long period. The record described his loneliness and stressed his aloofness. He happened to tell his housemaster of a former teacher who
had befriended him years before, and was astonished one
day to receive a visit from this same teacher, who apparently dropped in casually to see him. As a result of
repeated visits by this friend, a relationship was established between the boy and his housemaster which ultimately enabled the latter to effect a reconciliation between the boy and his father.

Governors make a point of personally greeting parents and friends who visit the institution. Housemasters
know of these calls in advance and are expected to be on
hand to talk over the cases of their boys. In the open institutions boys are encouraged to act as guides about the

place. Only the "browns" in the walled institutions are required to receive their visitors under supervision in a central administration building. On the annual field day, not only parents and friends of the boys, but interested visitors as well, are invited to witness the events and to inspect the institution. Parents visiting Hollesley Bay may stay week-ends at a nearby farmhouse and eat with their boys in the institution in a special visitors' room. At Camp Hill it has been found that allowing the boys a few short hours of liberty with their parents vacationing on the island produced a decidedly good effect on both parents and boys, and in no case has the privilege been abused.

For the last decade, the income from a fund of 10,000 pounds (a gift from Lord Nuffield) pays for transportation to and from the institution by parents who could not otherwise afford a visit. Because the income is not large, the privilege, however, cannot be extended more than once during the boy's term.

The institutions have experimented with a plan to allow some boys to visit their homes once during their term of training. A number of boys, carefully selected from each institution, are permitted home leave not exceeding five days, usually at Christmas or Easter. Home visits are also occasionally allowed at what is considered a vital point in the training of certain boys, at a time when they might otherwise go stale. Walled institutions as well as open institutions extend this opportunity to their boys, and it is stated that there has never been a single instance of failure to return to the institution. The institution pays their fare and allows a small sum for pocket money, both of these amounts also coming from the Nuffield Fund. A boy may make only one such visit in the course of his training. The Borstal Association first makes an investigation to see if the home is all right and if the family can afford to have the boy back for a few days. These visits are clearly seen to be an important way of keeping open a bridge between the institution and the outside world; through the visits the boys are enabled to establish new relationships with their families, looking forward to the time of their release. In connection with the home visits a chance is also given for visits to prospective employers.

Home visits are also made by housemasters. The Prison Commission allows each housemaster three or four days a year, salary and expenses paid, to enable him to visit some of the families of his boys. This practice is not as extensive as the Commission would like to have it, and it was planned, with increased staffs, to provide more time for such home visiting. One housemaster makes a point of visiting, on his own time, the home of each of his boys during his first three months at the institution. Housemasters set a high value on such home visits in the case of boys who present particularly difficult problems.

Community Relationships

Where a new Borstal Institution is not handicapped by inheriting a prison tradition, it has been found relatively easy to enlist the interest of the community in its development and in the welfare of individual boys. At Portland and Feltham, which had long been known, respectively, as a convict prison and a county industrial school, community support has been difficult, if not impossible, to arouse. At Rochester, however, the story has been different, perhaps because it was the first Borstal and elicited much interest. The newest institutions, North Sea Camp, Lowdham Grange, Hollesley Bay, and Usk, have been well accepted by their neighbors as local enterprises, and the boys have been made welcome as part of the community. In many Borstals lads are affiliated with outside organizations and when they are discharged they can continue as members of a local branch. Membership in such national organizations as the Sea Scouts or Toc H (an interdenominational social service group) and church bodies is an example of this policy.

No matter how forbidding the exterior of some of the former prison establishments may be, as Borstals they afford within their walls many features and conditions which are reminiscent of the outside world. Some institutions put on annual operettas, which draw patrons and audiences from the district. One Borstal has for years invited local girls to take the female rôles, and to rehearse, sing, and dance with the lads as members of the cast. Some institutions hold football matches and other sport competitions on their own grounds and invite outside teams.

Considerable ingenuity is evidenced in the schemes utilized; for example, one institution posts the results of school examinations on public boards not only in order to inform boys of their standing but for the additional reason that it is important to form the habit of looking at public notices in the outside world, a practice most Borstal boys have neglected.

One of the walled institutions over a period of years has developed, through personal contacts and by private arrangement, a corps of volunteer instructors each of whom comes out from town once a week to teach a wide variety of school, craft, and hobby classes. The institution provides transportation; otherwise the services of these teachers are rendered gratis. Newly established institutions particularly develop community interest by encouraging visitors at stated times. One governor says that he does not care whether they are really interested or just curious; the important thing is that they come to see, and he feels they are entitled to be shown. He assigns boys from the institution to act as guides, out of conscious recognition of the value to them of these outside contacts.

A definite reciprocal relationship exists between the institution and the community. All kinds of people from the outside world pass in and out of the institution— tradesmen, parents and friends of the boys, visitors, families of staff members, visiting athletic teams, dramatic groups, and teachers. The boys in the trusted classes also go out from the institution into the community at regulated periods for specified purposes. This controlled interaction between institutional life and the everyday life outside cannot be too strongly emphasized for a proper understanding of both the spirit and the method of Borstal training.

The open institutions as well as those of medium security allow boys in the blue class and the leavers to camp out with their housemasters during the summer. Each Borstal governor makes his own arrangements for camping facilities and a selected group is released under supervision for a week or two. Mornings at camp are given over to some kind of work to remunerate the owner of the site; afternoons and evenings are free for all kinds of informal activities and sports. All of the walled institutions regularly have parties of boys at work—farming, quarrying, and laboring outside the walls. One of the Borstals for serious offenders specializes in cross-country running with the coach, well beyond the bounds of the institution. It has already been noted that all Borstals make a practice of Sunday afternoon hikes, far from institution property.

Blue boys from a Borstal Institution only thirteen miles from London are allowed to attend moving picture shows once a month in the nearby town. They go in groups of four or six under the supervision of a housemaster or staff officer, pay for their tickets out of their own earnings, and are not looked at askance by the townspeople in the audience. The theater in a community where the local Borstal has established particularly good rapport with the town is open every Saturday afternoon free of charge for boys from the institution. Football teams and acrobatic and dramatic groups from this Borstal Institution take part in community affairs. At another institution, 120 boys, two-thirds of the total inmate body, have been enrolled in evening classes in the nearby town. Two groups of sixty alternated in attending each week. The local education authority cooperated by furnishing books and supplies. Free intermingling was allowed between the young people of the town, both boys and girls, and the boys from the institution. Boys from the Usk Borstal walked and rode through the town between prison and camp, and on summer evenings swam in the river at the same beach as the townspeople.

Borstal officials are solicitous about the impression made by their boys when they appear in public. One housemaster was severely criticized for allowing his lads to drink ale in a public house on the way back from a route march, not only because of possible objection on the part of parents but also because a wrong idea of Borstal was thus given to the outside world. Another housemaster was reprimanded for allowing his boys to swim nude in a river, even though he was convinced that they could not be seen. The governor stressed that boys should not be allowed to commit acts in the community which, even though unobserved, were nevertheless forbidden; such actions had an effect upon the boys themselves as well as on the public.

Borstal governors interpret the work of their institutions before all kinds of civic and religious groups. Support from voluntary sources is frequently forthcoming from the community in financial as well as social and educational ways. It has already been noted that approximately ten per cent of the budget of the Borstal Association is privately contributed; the donation by Lord Nuffield of 10,000 pounds has also been mentioned. Individual institutions are not infrequently the recipients of gifts from interested persons; one institution was given a complete moving picture projection room and all equipment by a local manufacturer; at another, townspeople subscribed 300 pounds to build a swimming pool; at still another, a service club raised in the community the necessary funds to transport Borstal lads to local football matches.

At each Borstal there is a Visiting Committee made up of not less than six local people, appointed by the Home Secretary, who interest themselves in the administration of the institution and act both as spokesmen for the community and guarantors of good standards of institutional management. They attend one official meeting monthly at the institution where they discuss questions of policy, serious problems of individual boys and, at least nominally, pass on lads for discharge. It is customary for each member of the Committee to make a particular house his special concern. He may supply funds for furnishings, radio, pictures, special sport equipment, parties and such luxuries. Some members also take a personal interest in individual boys and help to find employment for them before they are paroled. The Visiting Committee is recognized as an important means of drawing the community into a close relationship with the institution and an attempt therefore is made to have them represent, as far as possible, a cross section of the neighborhood.

Local support is recognized as necessary in the establishment of a new Borstal unit. After a site has been purchased and before any boys are selected or building operations are begun, members of the Prison Commission and the prospective governor make a trip to the community and talk with representative local townspeople— church leaders, school authorities, medical men, and other important groups and individuals. Letters of introduction to influential citizens living near the site of the proposed institution are secured from persons in other localities where Borstals are in operation. Volunteers are asked to give their time to teaching and related activities. Thus, even before it is under way, the idea has already spread through the town that here is something that will be worth watching and helping.

Since the trade unions play a more important rôle in the political and social life of Great Britain than they do in America, it is interesting to know how their cooperation has been secured. This was especially necessary in the construction of the more recent Borstal Institutions, which have been built almost exclusively by inmate labor. Misunderstandings and conflicts were obviated by consulting with the unions at the very inception of a new Borstal Institution. A plan was agreed upon in advance whereby the unions supplied a specified number of instructors from among their membership to every trade group of inmate workers. One of the institutions which has engaged in a very extensive building project costing upwards of a half million dollars, and has not yet after nine years completed its entire program, reports a complete absence of any difficulty with local unions by reason of the mutual understanding reached at the outset, and the observance of that agreement by both sides.

North Sea Camp developed a close relationship between its staff and inmate members and the historic community of Boston in a manner that is indeed unique in reformatory history. The townspeople were inclined to be suspicious of the new enterprise for the training of young criminals which was contemplated on the shore of The Wash, seven miles away. The first contingent of boys to arrive at the camp had it impressed upon them that they must maintain the good opinion created by the Prison Commissioners and the Borstal governor who visited the town before building operations were started. They were told, "If you escape, please don't steal a car in Boston or break into a house in Boston." Helpful contacts between town and Borstal were developed very slowly at first, but after the institution had been running a year, the resources of the town and the energies of local volunteers were freely placed at the disposal of the Camp.

It is only necessary to list the wide variety of activities in which town and institution at this Borstal share and the opportunities created for boys to meet local people, in order to show the high degree of cooperation effected between them. The county library furnished a new collection of books every six months; two volunteers teach baking and cabinet-making, respectively; a local architect instructs in mechanical drawing; a cobbler comes out to give lessons in simple shoe repairing; the musical society provides monthly concerts at the institution; an enthusiast in old English folklore holds classes in singing, poetry, and square dancing; the son of a famous explorer living near by leads a Toc H Club at the Camp; three hundred people from the town attend the annual sports day and the annual dramatic performance; a local football association invites the Borstal lads to their home games; the church reserves special pews for them; Borstal boys are asked to march with civic groups

in town parades; youth hostels offer their facilities for
week-end trips; local people invite those in the leavers'
grade to tea on occasional Sunday afternoons; a doctor
who volunteers to teach painting at the institution reserves one room in his home where housemasters may
always be assured of "dinner, whiskey, and a bed" on
their day off. Only two incidents have upset the har-
mony of this relationship with the community: a boy
stole a wheel for his bicycle while he was on a trip to
Boston; a parolee who came back to spend a few days
with a friend in the town stole some money from him.
The intensive development of the friendly spirit between town and institution has justified the imagination
and early efforts of those who first established the institution. The annual dinner at a local hotel given by the
governor of North Sea Camp for all those who aided
during the year was addressed by the Prison Commissioner, which helped greatly to encourage community
participation.

The community success of North Sea Camp may be
partly explained by the fact that it, like Lowdham, deals
with the presumably more responsive offenders committed to Borstal. The institution at Feltham, which receives the duller young criminal, has, however, also experimented with a project in community relationship
which suggests it is not so much the type of human material as the program and the way in which it is directed
that accounts for its success.

For three months in the summer of 1939, thirty boys
selected from the inmate group at Feltham lived and
worked in the old Reading Gaol which had been closed

in 1915. They spent their evenings and free time among the people of that city. This project called for hard monotonous labor—restoring the whole of the interior of this neglected institution to prepare it for a possible war emergency to house prisoners or enemy aliens.

Two housemasters, a disciplinary officer, a cook, and a painting foreman directed the work and leisure activities of these thirty youths. Staff and boys occupied the same quarters and shared a common mess. The division of hours was much the same as that at Feltham, except for the evening period. From 6 to 7 p.m. the boys were required to devote an hour to study or other quiet activity. Then after a clean-up there was a free period from 7:30 to 9:00 in the city of Reading or the nearby countryside. The gates were locked only during the day to keep out the curious; after work they stood open. All took advantage of the liberty to leave the institution during the evening, but they were not permitted to go about in groups larger than three. Two of the staff strolled through the town every night as proctors. The boys were free to talk with boys or men in the town but were not allowed to have any communications with girls. Those who violated any of these rules were "gated" for a week. Anyone who was not in by nine could not go out the following night, and the entire group as well was penalized by being required to return fifteen minutes earlier on the following night.

On Saturday, work ended at noon and the group was free. They returned by teatime, and had the evening free until nine. On Sunday mornings they attended church services, returned to the institution for early din-

ner, and in the afternoon split up under various leaders
to go on hikes. They took food with them for the evening meal and were away from the institution for a full
eight hours. As on other days, they were permitted to
lunch in cafés.

Weekday evenings were varied with a wide program
of activities in which local people shared. The YMCA
provided a gymnasium instructor; volunteers taught
crafts and directed games; the local Borstal Associate
gave a lecture on parole, and a doctor two talks on first
aid; a collection of books from the town library was
loaned; ministers from local churches met with their
communicants; the housemaster and his assistant carried
on interviews with their boys in preparation for discharge. Local clubs lent boxing gloves, a radio set, darts,
pingpong and billiard tables, but except during the free
time at noon these were little used.

Games and matches were held with outside organizations; church clubs arranged social evenings for the
boys; the town council gave permission for them to use
the public swimming pool without charge. One night a
week the group went *en masse* to a moving picture theater which gave them a special admission price. They
were paid at a slightly higher rate than at Feltham because their work was harder and because they required
somewhat more pocket money for their free time in the
town.

Two boys who were detained inside the prison awaiting transfer back to Feltham because of unsatisfactory
conduct got away, but it is a very interesting fact that no
escapes took place among those whose liberty was not

curtailed. After their three months' work was finished, an evening of entertainment for the local people who had cooperated so generously was provided by the boys before they returned to Feltham.

This experiment by an institution of medium security has been described in detail because it proves not only the possibility of a close relationship between institution and community, but also the value of such a relationship. It is another example of the willingness of the Borstal authorities to try a new departure even in an institution which has been operating for thirty years.

CHAPTER XII

THE WALLED BORSTALS

THE Borstal System includes five training institutions which, now largely reconstructed, were formerly prisons of the familiar penal appearance with cells, bars, locked gates, and walls. The units of this type —Rochester, Feltham, Portland, Sherwood, Camp Hill —receive, by and large, the tougher, older, more mature, and more difficult cases. Because many of the features of these institutions have been described under other headings in preceding chapters, no attempt will be made here to do more than give their general differentiating characteristics and facilities and to add some of the aspects of their operation which have not been previously considered.

Rochester

Rochester, the original Borstal Institution, opened officially in 1908. Located on the hills above the Medway River, it commands a fine view of the Kentish countryside. The inmate population averages between 350 and 400, a total which the governor deplores as being too large. The boys are distributed among five houses, each with its housemaster, assistant, matron, and two disciplinary officers. Four of the more recently built houses contain dormitories; the oldest was an original prison building with a central corridor and cells. The cells, now made into separate rooms, are quite colorful and cheerful, and are generally preferred to the dormitories. The whole atmosphere of the institution is made pleasant through playing fields, swimming pool, and well-tended flower gardens.

To Rochester are assigned older offenders of good intelligence, considered at the observation center to be in need of thorough trade training, combined with intensive supervision and personal help. Allocation to a particular house is carefully made on the basis of the special problems of the offender and the individual temperament and interests of the housemaster.

The staff members are given even more than the usual attention by the governor to make up for the small amount of time which he can give individually to so large a population. New housemasters live with their boys for the first three months. After this probationary period they may live apart from their group. Great emphasis is placed on a process of developing in each young inmate abilities and interests of which he may sometimes not have been aware. While each housemaster has the responsibility for his own house, he is also assigned some duty in another house in order to have an opportunity to know other boys besides his own. The relationships between staff and boys are enhanced by attracting staff members who have a broad range of interests and skills.

In this Borstal there are altogether thirteen trades taught, all in buildings with modern machinery and other equipment. For example, metal is forged and worked up from the raw material to the finished construction product for their own buildings and steel racks for government offices. The carpentry and joining include making furniture of good quality. Here as in some other Borstals a really thorough course in baking and cooking is given because there is a steady demand for hotel and sea cooks. A vocational test given shortly after arrival helps determine special ability or aptitude for a particular trade. A newcomer spends his first month in a reception class where he is expected to do the drudgery of maintenance work. At the end of this month he is transferred to a laboring group, until a vacancy occurs in the work party which he prefers or for which he has been found fitted.

Leisure to be used in a constructive way as a member of a club or craft group is regarded as an important privilege. The aim is to introduce the greatest possible number of hobbies and clubs to satisfy a wide variety of tastes and abilities. In a number of the shops the boys are allowed Saturday morning off from production work to make anything they want in their own way—calipers, micrometers, squares, punches, and the like—as long as they keep fully occupied.

There is not only much work but much freedom to go about the institution. Except at night, the entrances to the various houses are kept open for the boys to come and go as they need and to visit other houses in their free period. Some of the houses had been experimenting with keeping their gates open at night also, but the results of this experiment were undetermined when the war began.

Boys who are disciplinary problems are kept busy at made work arranged for them and are not allowed to share in the recreational program. They are regarded as being in need of added stimulus to exertion in order that they may have no time to brood or deteriorate and are therefore not locked up in solitary cells as may be done for very brief periods in some other Borstals.

Special attention is given to young men who have completed their training period in the "brown" grade in order to note that point in their development where it is believed that they are ready to be transferred to the "blue." There is equal care to recognize the point when the lad has absorbed a maximum of benefit and is naturally anxious to be out and away. The governor is a strong believer in the doctrine that there is a point in the training of each boy at which the institution has done him all the good it can; if allowed to remain too long beyond this point, he may begin to lose the impulse to try a new start in the community where he may apply the training he has received at Rochester.

Feltham

The institution at Feltham was the second taken over by the Prison Commission for development as a Borstal. It was formerly a county industrial school for boys, operated since 1854. Less than a mile from the town of Feltham and some thirteen miles from London, the institution is located in a district specializing in the growing of flowers and seeds. An eight-foot wall encloses a large part of its 96 acres of grounds, with several gates which are left open and unguarded. During the past three years, the average population has been between 350 and 400 boys.

In September, 1939, at the beginning of the war, the

authorities took advantage of the changing situation to transfer to Feltham the observation center formerly at Wormwood Scrubs, in order to remove it entirely from a prison atmosphere.

Allocation was made to Feltham chiefly on the basis of mental dullness or the need for special physical attention. This was done for various reasons, among them that Feltham was one of the few institutions with a full-time physician, that it was well equipped with hospital facilities and a solarium, that it was not far from London specialists and consultants. It is realized that there are certain objections to grouping young men together on the basis of a particular mental or physical defect, but as an administrative matter it is believed better to concentrate these two groups in one institution than to scatter them through the other eight units. It is further recognized that some of the boys with physical difficulties may exert a certain leavening effect on the other elements in the institution, particularly the mentally dull, and that some of the former may even derive a certain compensatory satisfaction from their mental superiority.

The physical training program at Feltham aims at building up the health and strength of the boys under the direction of three full-time physical education instructors, trained at Aldershot. All new arrivals must undergo two months of specialized exercise for an hour a day, five days a week. This includes outdoor gymnastics and individual corrective work. The regular afternoon drill is varied with boxing, wrestling, track, swimming instruction, diving, and so on.

A stay at Feltham convinces the visitor that the insti-

tution is extraordinarily well run. The continuous operation of this institution for the past thirty years as a Borstal, with a staff that has long been connected with it, and
the steady routine undoubtedly conduce to the stabiliza-
tion of the problem youths committed to it for treatment
and training. The needs of this same group probably account also for a rather rigid adherence to the brown and
blue ratings and the partial dependence upon inmate
leaders for the maintenance of discipline. The treatment
in the largest percentage of cases is to supply the kind
of training, particularly habit training, that the lads allocated here have always lacked and from which the
mentally dull particularly profit. Therefore the average
length of time spent at this institution is greater than at
any other Borstal. About eighteen months elapse in most
cases before promotion from the brown grade to the
greater privilege and responsibility of the blue, and the
training period will be found to run somewhat over,
rather than under, two years.

The growing of chrysanthemums, tomatoes, and other
hothouse plants is a specialty at Feltham, and many boys
trained in this work easily find jobs when they are
discharged. Most work at Borstal Institutions is done
for governmental departments, but the above products
are sold in the open market in competition with other
growers.

Portland

Portland was taken over by the Prison Commission in
1921 to serve as the third Borstal Institution. Formerly
an old convict prison, south of Weymouth in Dorset-

shire, it more closely resembles the penitentiary type of institution than any of the other Borstal units. It houses 350 young men. The situation of Portland on a peninsula connected by a narrow isthmus to the mainland makes escape difficult. Older and tougher offenders are allocated here, the average age on admission running close to twenty-one years.

Despite the external grimness of this institution and its location on the farthest point of a high and rocky promontory, there is now much more to remind the visitor of a Borstal than of a prison. Flower beds inside and outside the walls, the absence of locks on cells or bars on doors during the day, the civilian dress of the officers and housemasters, are as much features of this institution as of the most open Borstal camp, despite the character and antecedent behavior of its inmates.

Great stress is laid here upon physical training and development because of the softness of many of the incomers and their need for the disciplinary values of such measures. Individual cards of height, weight, and measurement are kept for each man. Mirrors placed about the gymnasium help to emphasize the value of good posture and "form" in gymnasium and acrobatic work. Three physical training instructors give full time to the athletic program, facilities for which include two very fine sport grounds, formerly abandoned quarries which over a period of years have been filled in and graded by institution labor. Almost a third of the institution's sixty-eight acres is devoted to playing fields. Acrobatic work is highly developed at Portland; young men anxious to become proficient beyond the regular physical training programs may join a gymnastic club, to which they must pay dues out of their weekly earnings.

The tempo and atmosphere of this institution reflect the dynamic personality of its governor who seems capable of infusing both staff and inmates with an energy and enthusiasm that are as difficult to describe as they are infectious. The buoyancy and jollity of this man in his relationships, even disciplinary, with the lads are most striking. This is one of the few Borstals where any real attempt is made to call the inmates by their given names.

The personnel realize that the task of attempting to reconstruct the attitudes of these older offenders, all of whom will have reached more than their majority upon their release, is no simple matter. Young men who have been in and out of reform schools, who may have had a previous jail or Borstal experience, who have been deserters from the various armed services, are not easily reformed. The regime at Portland depends a great deal, as it must at all such institutions, upon the effect of a daily routine. To this is added the thorough course in physical rebuilding mentioned above. Two additional factors, the energy of the staff and the initiation of supervised work programs outside the institution walls a few months before release, are other notable characteristics distinguishing Portland from other Borstals.

Sherwood

Sherwood, it will be recalled, was chosen for an early experiment with older recidivists, the success of which led to the increase in the Borstal age from twenty-one to twenty-three years. Like the other four-walled institutions, it was formerly a prison. Situated on a hill within the city limits of Nottingham, Sherwood receives the oldest group allocated for Borstal training, those between the ages of twenty-one and twenty-three, with an average roll of one hundred and fifty. Because the institution often has to hold those committed to it for three years, Sherwood has some men as old as twenty-five and twenty-six. It has been described as "a Borstal for the twenties rather than a Borstal for the teens." While inmates at other Borstals may be called "lads," here they are definitely referred to as "men," dressed in long trousers instead of the traditional shorts which are seen at other institutions. As already indicated, gradings are based on length of training. Blues are allowed a short distance outside the institution only under supervision, specifically to work at reclamation of land owned by the institution which is being prepared for use as athletic fields.

The most important trade taught here is wood-working. Instruction is also given in building and allied trades by the construction of some new staff quarters, inmate-built, and the upkeep of the plant. The shops are equipped with the latest type of power machinery and tools. As in other Borstals, the time spent within the institution is not always adequate for a thorough trade training comparable to a completed apprenticeship in the outside world, but it is continued long enough to enable the worker to reach at least the rank of "improver," a level recognized in the trades. Through being taught the use of up-to-date methods and equipment, men released from Sherwood should not have great difficulty in securing positions in modern industry.

Because of the age and background of the men at this institution, it is essential to maintain a strict level of discipline. Offenders who are allocated here often display an initial bitterness at receiving a three-year Borstal term where an ordinary prison sentence might have seen them free much sooner. Locks and bars are a more common feature than at other Borstals, and all men sleep in individual cells. Stone-breaking for men in the "penal class" has been abolished in recent years and sawing up of old railroad ties (with a dull saw) has been substituted. The retention of this punitive device is described as necessary because on occasion these men must be dealt with firmly.

A large proportion of the men allocated to Sherwood have already served a prison sentence; many of them are married. Here the governor is particularly careful in the type of matron selected for the service and older women are chosen. The more closely personal relationship which is found at the Borstals for younger offenders is not countenanced here. Nevertheless a sympathetic attitude toward the men is encouraged, and housemasters work more closely with their matrons because of the important influence the latter may have upon a class of men who, due to their age and repeated institutional commitments, are difficult to reach.

New arrivals at Sherwood are assigned by rote to one of the three sections or houses which make up the institution; individualized work is made possible by having one housemaster to about forty men. The three sections may spend their free time together, but they are separated for meals and other group activities. The compactness of the institution makes possible a close acquaintance of each housemaster with his men. Each section is further divided into three groups of about fifteen each. The plan here is to have the men in their cells only during the night, and only in their house at meal times; the rest of the day they are at work in the shops or fields, and they spend their free time in a separate building equipped for games and other leisure-time activities. The average stay is slightly over two years.

Camp Hill

The fifth Borstal to be established, Camp Hill, was formerly a prison for habitual offenders, located near Newport on the Isle of Wight. It is a walled institution with six houses and accommodates approximately 350 youths. The famous convict prison of Parkhurst lies in a valley below the rise on which Camp Hill is located. The institution receives the young but hardened offenders, those with previous institutional experience, deserters and other ex-service men, and especially young automobile thieves. Escape from the institution is next to impossible because of the island location. The average age on admission here is nineteen, and the number of previous convictions averages four.

The authorities at Camp Hill clearly recognize that the former experiences of these young men militate against the success of any attempt to arouse them by the means used with less criminally sophisticated offenders. The idea of group spirit and group loyalties has been served up to many of them as a mass gospel when they were younger, and has evidently failed. It is realized that any reformation which is to be effective with this particular group must be brought about by other methods. For these reasons, an intensive program of individual interviews is in operation here. While the process is not labeled by any technical term, what is attempted here partakes somewhat of the nature of a psychiatric procedure. It is believed that if these young lawbreakers can be made to engage in self-analysis, they may be brought to realize that the faults in their attitude and outlook are the basic reasons for their failure.

A secret society, whose name and purpose are undefined and none of whose members know one another, is composed of carefully selected young men who put their signatures to a roster, below those of other lads whose names are concealed when a new name is added. Only the lads who have joined, the chaplain, and the governor know of the existence of the society, and only these last two officials know all who have signed the parchment. When the lad seems to have made some progress in his talks with his housemaster, he is seen by the governor. After several interviews, the latter asks him if he would like to sign his name to whatever unspoken pledges he cares to make to himself. There are no initiations, dues, or meetings of this group. It represents a conscious attempt on the part of the governor to capitalize on the propensities of adolescents to be egocentric and introspective. The self-examination of these lads in their meetings with the housemaster and governor is believed by this governor to be a very effective way of reaching them, of exerting a personal influence that may have lasting effects.

Meetings at which lads are considered for release are made very serious occasions. Every case must be acted upon three months before discharge may take effect; the record of each boy is presented by his housemaster at a meeting of all housemasters, the governor, and his deputy. The housemaster then calls in the young man who is told that he is being considered for release. He is asked to give reasons both for and against it. The housemaster may act as his counsel if he cares to, or may contribute nothing to the examination unless he is requested to do so by the governor or asked by the boy himself. These meetings go into great detail; the lad may be expected to defend his actions in the institution, or to outline the plan he has for himself after discharge. Any member of the group may ask a question, defend or disapprove the discharge. Of thirty-three cases considered at a meeting which lasted for three days, only eleven were approved for release. The proceedings appear to be rather gruelling affairs, but it must be remembered that they climax a period of training in which great stress has been laid upon intensive work with the young offender, in which self-criticism and the discussion of personal problems and individual attitudes have been made the basis for reformation.

The two Borstal units actually within prison walls naturally have to abide by the general prison regulations and are supervised by the prison governors. Each, how-

ever, occupies a building entirely separate from the
other prison population and is under the direct management of a Borstal housemaster.

The Observation Center

While in each recent year about 1,000 lads have been
collected for observation and study in a wing of Wormwood Scrubs Prison the average number awaiting allocation at any one time is only about seventy. They occupy
two tiers of cells made over into rooms, the central corridor serves for dining room and quiet recreations. There
is a library. Within certain limits outdoors the boys are
free to roam about at regulated times. There is a little
work for them to do about the grounds and some effort
is made at academic tasks. Good discipline is maintained
and there is close oversight of the boys. It seems doubt-
ful whether any specific harm is done to them by their
confinement which is seldom more than a month, but
there has long been the desire on the part of the Borstal
authorities to separate this period of observation from
prison surroundings. The outbreak of war saw the realization of this.

In the boys' prison at Wormwood Scrubs, separate
from the observation center, a number of Borstal cases
have been held for varying times during a recent four-
year period to ascertain what could be achieved by professional psychotherapy. The selection of these 63 lads
was made from parole "revokees," from among those
who had proved themselves aggressively antisocial or
otherwise abnormal in a training Borstal, or they were
referred for treatment as the result of investigations at

the observation center. The outcome of the psycho-therapeutic approach will be mentioned in the chapter dealing with evaluation of the Borstal System.

The Borstal Unit at Wandsworth Prison

All those reconvicted of offenses during the four-year period of Borstal control, all who have broken parole by reason of persistent poor conduct of other kinds, and those exceptional lads who have been found impossible to handle by the ordinary disciplinary methods of the training institutions are collected in a special wing of Wandsworth Prison where they are under their own housemaster but are subject to the ordinary prison regime. A special board meets monthly to reconsider all the cases assigned to Wandsworth during the month. The average number of cases to be passed on is fifteen.

Previous to the hearing the revokees have been interviewed by the housemaster and the Director of the Borstal Association—the latter because he is particularly interested to know why his parole agents or the Associates have failed with any given boy. The board consists of the Director, the Wandsworth housemaster, two lay members, and the Commissioner in charge of the Borstal System who presides. Sometimes there is also present a governor of some particular Borstal. At the meeting the boy is interviewed and his record considered.

There are some very definite limitations to what the board may prescribe in the case. If it is found that a judge has given a sentence which extends for a longer period than the remainder of the four years during which there is Borstal control, the offender must serve that prison sentence and the case need not be considered. Usually, however, except for serious offenses, the court has given a nominal short sentence in order that the Borstal authorities may make their own decision. In any such case, however, control of the boy cannot be retained beyond the four-year period.

The decision frequently is a sentence to the Borstal Wing of Wandsworth for three or four months. Then if the period of Borstal control is not completed the boy is again paroled. Or occasionally he may be re-paroled directly after the hearing. Also, of course, it is possible to return him to the institution from whence he came, or transfer him to another Borstal. Or the boy may be held at Wandsworth until his entire Borstal period is ended. The group accumulated through all these different types of dispositions leads to a daily average population of about one hundred.

CHAPTER XIII

THE OPEN BORSTALS

THE last decade has seen the introduction into the Borstal System of unwalled and unfenced institutions. Such units, now numbering four—Lowdham Grange, North Sea Camp, Hollesley Bay, and Usk—represent the most progressive development of English training methods for the youthful offender. The fact has already been noted that allocations to these four institutions are made on the basis of likelihood of response to conditions of limited freedom; those who prefer a walled institution to the acceptance of the responsibility which such freedom demands are not sent to an open institution. With the establishment of North Sea Camp in 1935, the Prison Commission accepted the principle of "camp" training—frankly borrowed from America, but carried much farther and extensively varied in form. While there are many exceptions, as may be seen from our outline of the scheme of allocation, in general Lowdham Grange and the three camp Borstals accept for treatment the younger, less mature, and presumably more readily reformable types of offenders. Differences among these four institutions are given in some detail below.

Lowdham Grange

Lowdham Grange was the first Borstal to be established *de novo* and apart from prison structures, such as

those in which all the walled institutions had their beginnings. As has been noted, its establishment was carefully provided for—staff and boys lived together for six
months and planned the new venture before setting out
on the march to the new site. The construction of all of
the houses, staff quarters, gymnasium, administration
and service buildings, including the plumbing, electrical
equipment, and interior decoration, has been the work of
the boys themselves, under the direction of expert crafts-
men who served as instructors and foremen. The need
for trained workers in the building and affiliated trades
and the desire to enter into this field are among the factors taken into consideration for allocation to Lowdham
Grange, although farming and the care of a herd of pure-
bred cattle and other farm animals also occupy the attention of some proportion of the inmate group.

Three extremely well-built brick and stone houses,
connected by elevated tiled terraces, accommodate about
180 boys. Another under construction will make possible the allocation here of 250, the maximum number
contemplated. The gate posts flanking the entrance to
the institution bear no identifying sign or tablet and no
gate, open or shut, swings between them. The magnifi-
cent sweep of the institution buildings across the crest
and down the side of a hill overlooking the wooded
country a few miles from Nottingham gives the appearance of a fine, modern, preparatory school. There are no
walls, no window bars, nor is there any locking up. Restraints upon the movement of the lads within the institution during free time are few.

Lowdham Grange was the first institution to introduce the serving of food in cafeteria style, which is said to make for less waste, better manners, and a generally freer and more natural atmosphere at meals. As at all other Borstals, talking among inmates is allowed at all times, whether at table, work, or play. The only restraint is imposed at the "silent hours," when studying or class work is going on. The boys sleep in large, airy dormitories that occupy the full length of each house.

Matrons and boys are encouraged to do much in the way of arrangement and adornment of their houses. Curtains, flowers, pictures, radios, bulletin boards, game rooms provide an attractive and informal setting for indoor activities when work is over. Lowdham Grange allots a small plot of land to each boy for the cultivation of vegetables and flowers for his own use or for sale to members of the institution staff.

The chief concern of the governor and his staff is to give each boy a sense of accomplishment—the learning of a trade is considered secondary to the satisfaction expected to come from the creation, bit by bit according to plans, of sections, floors, and finally an entire building.

The cost and finances of the buildings are thought to have been justified by the standard of skills acquired in their construction. It is the idea of the governor that when completed this unit should be sold and another one started. The goal of the project would be reached with the ending of the building program. But an alternative plan has been suggested, namely, that with the completion of the four housing units, work shops for intensive trade training might be built and the whole institution be continued as a Borstal unit.

North Sea Camp

North Sea Camp is perhaps the most novel and interesting of recent Borstal experiments, and represents the
greatest possible departure from conventional reformatory method. Six miles from Boston, Lincolnshire, this
Borstal unit is situated near the marsh bordering the bay
known as The Wash. The one-story buildings of the
Camp are constructed of corrugated iron and concrete,
with finished interiors. In appearance, North Sea Camp
resembles a neatly laid out, semi-permanent construction camp.

In this instance, appearance bespeaks function, for the
project of the Camp is the reclamation of the salt marsh
from the tides and storms which pound in from the
North Sea. Since the days when the Romans built a high
bank which still runs for forty miles up the coast, this
part of the country has been noted for its rich farm land.
A large part of the soil which is tilled today in this re-
gion was once under water. Practically the only labor at
North Sea Camp is the work of reclaiming additional
acres from the sea and the building of dikes to protect
them. In this struggle against nature it was expected
that hardihood would be developed as an important part
of the training and, as more land was brought under
cultivation, a feeling of achievement for England. The
truth of the latter was demonstrated in 1939 by the
great enthusiasm displayed in the first small harvest
from an experimental plot of wheat, cabbage, and pota-
toes, the result of four years of labor.

North Sea Camp accommodates 120 boys, all but ten
per cent of whom are engaged during their working

hours in labor on the marshes. All told, the staff numbers twenty-two, of whom nine are housemasters and two are matrons. Unlike other Borstals, it has no disciplinary staff. The housemasters—and frequently the governor—toil with the boys, wash and eat with them, share their evening activities, and sleep in the same dormitories. North Sea Camp comes nearer to being a communal type of organization than any other Borstal. Selection here, as in the other open Borstals, is based first on likelihood of response to freedom. The boys who are sent here are largely those who chose to engage in heavy physical labor, or those who already have some vocational skill at command and so need no special training. It is acknowledged that North Sea Camp receives the most promising of all the Borstal lads. Like Lowdham Grange and Usk, it does not accept those who are unwilling to take a pledge "to keep up the good name" of the institution.

During the first eighteen months the buildings were set up and equipped by the boys working with artisans. During the following two and one-half years, one hundred and eighty acres were reclaimed. The strenuous life leaves little opportunity for planned interviews with the housemasters that is so much a feature of other Borstals. Much the same result is secured by having the staff share fully in the daily life. Their personal influence is a continuous process fifteen hours of the day—at meals, at work, during classes and recreation periods. But every boy is called in by the governor for a personal talk at least three times a month.

The cooperation of the neighboring community of

Boston in the enterprise has already been told in detail. The impact of outside talent was a carefully planned feature of the institution from the start. An extraordinary variety of activity fills the free periods: foreign languages are taught by the linguaphone method; amateur meteorological and regional surveys are made; every boy is taught how to wash and mend his own clothes and repair his own shoes; a dam built by the boys across a creek provides a swimming hole; they hike, camp, and explore the neighboring country and sail up and down the coast, some of them as a company of Sea Scouts.

Life here is made not only strenuous but exciting for active boys in their late teens. The ordinary indoor amusements and games are deliberately lacking in order to teach these young men that there are other pursuits that have a long-range value. Each man selected to serve on the staff of the Camp is expected to have one dominant interest or hobby which he communicates to and shares with the boys. Because the workday is vigorous, privileges and opportunities are allowed which are unknown in other Borstals.

Work on the salt marshes goes on five and one-half days a week, regardless of cold, tide, or wind. Four hours of work in the morning are interrupted only by a half-hour for lunch, eaten at a special hut set up at the work site. Newcomers spend the first month doing maintenance work around the institution; the rest of the boys do no other work than that with pick, shovel, and cart— digging up the heavy marsh soil, building up dikes and cross walls which keep out the sea. Boys work in gangs and are paid in accordance with the gang output. This practice is aimed at teaching the values of cooperative effort. A civil engineer directs the work; he has come to find that his job relates as much to the successful physical and personality development of the boys engaged in the project as it does to the progress of the project itself.

After a lad has been at the Camp for three months, the institution board meets to discuss his case. These first months are expected to see the boy through the "beginners' grade," in which he attends special classes. If considered fit for advancement at the end of this period, he is promoted to the "training grade." He is now expected to do his work and meet the requirements of his daily life largely on his own responsibility. After six months in this training grade, he goes into the leavers' grade in which he is allowed to go into town and on trips alone, and is generally trusted as ordinary people are. A high standard of individual development is maintained, the aim being to encourage self-reliance as rapidly as the individual can assume it.

North Sea Camp was designed to be a rigorous place, with a full day of struggle and accomplishment. Hard work is the main emphasis of the institution plan and routine. A definite feeling is created that here is a place where a sense of striving and of high personal achievement is fostered. The elements are the constantly advancing foe; the building of a dike against these elements is the daily battle. It was intended that the young men sent here for training should have a year of strenuous exertion, with its due reward, to look back upon. It was expected that, for many, the time spent at North Sea

Camp should be the fullest and most adventurous year
of their lives and it is learned that many boys remember it as such.

Hollesley Bay

By comparison with North Sea Camp, the colony at
Hollesley Bay, opened in 1938, seems tame and coun-
trified. Its main pursuits are those of the farm, orchard,
and greenhouse in addition to animal husbandry. The
whole is a colony with many features of a little village.
The central administration building has facilities for 150
colonists, and plans call for the erection of separate
houses situated within a three-quarter-mile radius from
the center. Since the type of lad allocated to Hollesley
Bay is also expected to respond favorably to freedom,
the institution has no walls or fences to mark it off from
the heath which surrounds it. Boys who come from agri-
cultural districts or who have an aptitude for or an interest in farming as an occupation are sent here. A collection of pets is maintained—rabbits, hares, ducks, chick-
ens, pigeons, geese—to accustom the boys to look upon
animals as a source of interest and pleasure, rather than
as targets.

The 1,300 acres of the colony give the advantage of
privacy. Boys who have passed through the beginner's
stage are allowed to work alone in the fields and or-
chards. Every boy has the privilege of his own locker.
The atmosphere of the institution is that of a large cooperative farm colony, well ordered and pleasant. Great
latitude is allowed the inmates in the choice of work and
avocational interests. Small fees are required for en-

trance into some of the craft and working clubs. During the harvest season, of course, all hands are expected to turn to and help get in the crop. Meetings of housemasters and governor are held daily. Stress is laid on inmate group discussions; topics relating to community life— "What is unemployment insurance?" "How is the town governed?" "How is the country governed?" are subjects discussed at group forums. The bulletin board outside one of these discussion rooms gives the subject for the night's meeting with the additional notation, "Walk in if you want to."

The "route march" or hike which is part of the Sunday program of every Borstal is a special club activity at Hollesley Bay. It is not compulsory but those who care to may join the Marchers' Club for which they pay a very small weekly sum. They walk from sixteen to thirty miles in a day, later taking turns at writing up the report of the trip for the club minutes. The governor's wife sometimes accompanies the boys and helps some of them with sketching. The club invites an occasional special guest—historian, military man, or explorer—to go with them.

The governor here favors a large institution—as far as both numbers and plant are concerned. He believes there is an advantage in a variety of inmates and in "open spaces" because of the opportunity for the boys to "lose themselves," both in their work and in their surroundings. The governor here also has the unusual idea that where there is a large number of individuals, a boy must wait to have a grievance considered by a housemaster or governor. A period of waiting allows a chance for temper to cool, for sober reflection. In the outside world, it is pointed out, one must wait to have his complaints heard or remedied.

Hollesley Bay is geared to a definite term of fifteen months for each lad. In this respect it is frankly experimental and differs from any of the other Borstals. Results were being watched very carefully. A boy is in the blue grade as soon as he arrives, and is granted all the privileges he will ever have. Fines are the only form of punishment, except, of course, an additional stay of one or more months for serious misbehavior, or transfer to another institution of greater security. The staff here talk in terms of "dissolving resentments" through the calm and well-ordered life of the colony. As elsewhere, boys are often tense and hostile when they are first received, but no attempt is made to deal with these attitudes until the regime of the institution has built up the boy physically and the simple way of country life has begun to make itself felt.

After his first month or two, the lad begins to open up, to ask advice, to seek for help through conversation with his housemaster or at the discussion groups. Intensive individual work begins at this point and interviews continue until the boy is ready for discharge. The colony council or "Moot," composed of the boys themselves, holds meetings at which suggestions are made and passed on to the administration. Suggestions accepted by the governor are embodied in the institution program and are looked upon as "agreements" fully entered into by staff and boys, and, like the pledge not to escape, they are accepted as a matter of trust and personal responsibility.

Usk

Most recent of the Borstal Institutions, Usk was established to care for the increased numbers of boys committed for Borstal training. The old prison, closed since 1922, in this Welsh town was taken over and with it were purchased some two hundred and fifty acres of scrub land, two and one-half miles away. This tract is the site of a camp where boys engage in clearing operations to prepare the land for agriculture. When the camp is completed, there are to be approximately one hundred boys there, and a somewhat smaller number at Usk. Allocations are made from among those considered for the open institutions but generally of a lower grade of intelligence. Little trade instruction is given other than in connection with the repair of the old prison structure and the remodeling necessary to convert it to its new use as a Borstal.

The first three months are spent in initial training at the prison building. This period serves a dual purpose—to accustom the boy to institutional routine and discipline and to estimate the likelihood of his adjustment to the conditions of camp life. Those who do not respond well are not sent up to camp, but are returned for reallocation. Lads at the camp who do not adjust there are returned to Usk for further training, and the repeated failures are sent to another Borstal. In the first six months of operation, only one recalcitrant lad and two absconders had to be transferred. In the early days such natural responses to the environment as trespassing on adjoining farms and setting snares for rabbits were not considered serious enough offenses to warrant transfer.

The spirit built up later led to the cessation of such activities.

In the old prison building the boys live in made-over cells and are occupied almost wholly within the grounds. Cells are never locked, and except at night the prison gates stand open. Life at the camp is varied and strenuous. Work parties are busy with road making, timber felling and clearing, quarrying, reservoir construction, fence making, and the setting of foundations for the erection of the prefabricated cabins which are to replace the tents in which the boys spent their first summer at the camp. While some of the boys allocated to Usk come from the Welsh countryside, the majority have been brought up in cities. They say the camp is a revelation to them—they thought that it would be dull, that they would miss the streets and the movies. Camp life was purposely designed to show these boys the variety of activities which country life affords. Spare time activities include horseback riding, canoeing, bicycling, hiking, visits to local historical sites, fishing, trips on canal boats.

The aim is to make the camp a place where boys will learn things by and for themselves. They are sent there when they can be expected to manage themselves and not be constantly shepherded. The life invites activity in the out-of-doors, and a spirit of self-reliance and hardihood is encouraged. Work and a full program of activities continue in all weathers. The deputy governor in charge thinks that an ideal of toughness appeals to most boys in their late teens and that if it is the right kind of toughness, it is a very good thing for them. His experience proves that it is so and he believes that heightened self-respect and self-reliance will stand them in good stead during later life.

Usk operates on the theory that insufficient emphasis has been placed by reformative methods on this factor of self-direction. The governor, who earlier organized the North Sea Camp, introduced here, too, the principle of developing character through encouraging the ability to maintain a daily program in the face of discomfort and even hardship. The boys build the canoes in which they learn to paddle, set up their own sport equipment, repair the leaks in their tents, cut their firewood, cook their own meals. Many of these experiences will perhaps never be repeated in later years, but they offer ways in which a boy's life is considerably enriched. Camp life is a new mode of existence for them. Eighteen months of institutional and camp training are expected to give them resourcefulness and stability which are likely to keep them from recruiting the ranks of adult criminals when they return to the community.

Unfortunately, the coming of the war has made it necessary to postpone the day when we might know more positively how successful were the results of the training at Usk.

CHAPTER XIV

THE BORSTAL ASSOCIATION

IN order to make clear the working methods of the Borstal System it has been necessary in the foregoing pages to refer to the Borstal Association, the parole agency which, in the interest of released Borstal lads, functions in such remarkably thoroughgoing fashion.[1] Before we discuss the diverse aspects of the efforts made for after-care some account of the organization itself is in order.

As stated earlier, the Borstal Association was formed in 1904 through private sponsorship. From the first recognized as vital to the success of Borstal training, this important department of the Borstal System is officially staffed under the direction of the Prison Commission and is now financially supported to only a small extent by private subscriptions. In recent years the budget of the Association has amounted to the equivalent of over sixty thousand dollars a year. The public subscribes about five thousand dollars each year and "each pound given earns a government subsidy of up to three pounds in addition to certain items which are entirely met by the government."

Corresponding to the area covered by the Borstal System, all of England and Wales is served by the Asso-

1. Throughout this and the next chapter, the word "parole" will be used in place of the English term "release on licence."

The Borstal Association does not handle the cases of girls. In April, 1928, their supervision was transferred to an After-Care Committee of the Borstal Institution for Girls at Aylesbury.

ciation. Its headquarters are in London, presided over by the Director who came to his position after fifteen years of experience in Borstal Institutions. In the London office his staff consists of twenty-five full-time paid officials. In Liverpool there is another office with a much smaller number of paid workers. The districts not covered by these two offices are supervised by the Provincial Department of the Association, headed by a deputy and executive secretary both of whom have been with the organization for many years.

In the London and Liverpool areas the staff members of the offices are in charge of parolees and their duties are similar in nature to those of parole officers in this country. In the "provinces," which include all other districts and, of course, many cities, the parole work is done by what are termed Official Borstal Associates.

The majority of these are probation officers specially appointed as official Associates and paid by the Association for the extra work which they do for Borstal parolees. In some instances, the probation officer who acts as the official Associate may earlier have had the lad on probation. While this may prove to be an advantage, in that it provides a continuity of acquaintance and interest, it also sometimes happens that the Borstal parolee gets the second-best efforts of the probation officer in the securing of jobs and so on, because his current probationers have first claim on his time and attention. For this reason the present administration of the Association is interested in securing persons other than probation officers to serve as official Associates.

It has been possible to obtain the services of carefully

selected professional people and others who have been engaged in some form of social work as official Associates, but so far these are outnumbered by the probation officers who take on the extra task. Teachers, ministers, physicians, and former army men are among the others most frequently appointed.

Still further assistance is rendered the parolees by the so-called Borstal Voluntary Associates who serve specifically in a friendly rather than in an official relationship to the lads and their families. These volunteers help to provide leisure-time activities and social contacts, and often aid in finding employment.

From its early days the Association has developed an organization of voluntary Associates. Over the years various sources have been tapped to find responsible people for this work; many have been secured from the churches; adult education centers have been consulted, for example, when voluntary Associates were needed in a remote section of the country. Through the national offices of their organizations suitable members of the St. Vincent de Paul Society and of a Jewish association are frequently found who are willing to become voluntary Associates for paroled lads in their home towns. Many valuable volunteer Associates have been developed who have continued their interest and service for years, while those who proved incapable or unsuited have gradually been dropped.

In total there are now over one thousand voluntary Associates distributed throughout England and Wales.

It thus appears that in most cases a released Borstal lad finds two people interested in him: his parole agent if he lives within the area of the two large cities named, or his local official Associate, and one other person who is presumed to take over the friendly and advisory rôle earlier assumed by his housemaster. One interesting example of the latter group is that of a voluntary Associate in a large manufacturing center, a physician, who has shown devotion to this work in a high degree. He has made a point of visiting at least once every Borstal boy from his city at whatever institution the lad happened to be in training. The release of large numbers from the Borstal Institutions at the outbreak of the present war increased his immediate case load to fifty. His spirit has so pervaded his own home life that even his housekeeper has become an active worker with the families of parolees.

Another activity of the Borstal Association has been the establishment of Borstal Voluntary Committees, which particularly include representatives of fraternal, business, trade, and religious groups. The spread of the idea of service for Borstal parolees has resulted in the formation of committees with membership from 348 different organizations in 44 communities. The function of these committees is to interpret to the public the work of the Borstal Association and to encourage their members or others to become voluntary Associates. This development is regarded as so important that one member of the central office staff devotes half of his time to stimulating the formation of Borstal Voluntary Committees and guiding their policies. Either the Director or this staff member meets each committee twice a year at its monthly meetings in order to advise on general procedure and to review every case in the district with the paroled lad's voluntary or official Associate. This connection of the Associate with a committee seems to have distinct advantages.

Personal contact between the main office of the Borstal Association and individual Associates, either official or voluntary, is an important part of the work of the organization. Associates often visit the London headquarters. The voluntary nature of a large part of this work makes necessary the supervision of a full-time staff member to assure standards and continuity to the service. As an example of the amount of work done at the head office it may be stated that over 25,000 letters, "many of them involving much time and thought," are sent out yearly. The Director of the Borstal Association describes his job as that of a case supervisor, and he frequently interests himself in particular cases even to the point of making home visits in order to "keep his hand in," lest his duties reduce themselves too completely to administrative routine.

Collaboration between the institution and the aftercare organization is not limited to the monthly visit by an agent of the Association to each institution. It has already been noted that housemasters annually spend three or four days at the Borstal Association office reviewing the cases of former boys, some of whom they visit at their homes. Housemasters and governors on coming to London frequently drop in at the Association office. Previous acquaintance of Borstal Association officials with present governors of institutions makes for a personal and harmonious relationship between the two staffs. District conferences are held from time to time with Associates and institution officials present to discuss methods for improving their joint services. The annual meetings of Borstal governors and housemasters are attended also by the Borstal Association staffs. In these ways the recognized tendency of all institutions to draw away from the outside world is partly offset, and at the same time the parole organization has opportunity to become acquainted with changing institutional procedures and their implications for parole work.

The Association informs the institution of the subsequent conduct of each of its graduates by means of a review sent twice yearly, giving the parolee's present whereabouts and describing his occupation, attitude, and activities. This follow-up report (called a "flimsy" from the nature of the paper used) is sent to the institution from which final discharge was made. The institution appends these "flimsies" to the record of each former inmate.

The Borstal Associates, either official or voluntary, are required to send a notice of the boy's arrival at his home and again when he is settled at work. Thereafter they report once a month on his progress, unless he loses his job, behaves unsatisfactorily, or drops from sight, in which case they are required to communicate at once with the head office. One of the most noteworthy bits of parole procedure is that found in the practice of the Director who reviews the record of every boy on parole in the London area once a week to discover what steps recommended during the past seven days have not been taken. He described various "tickler" systems formerly used, but states that he has discarded them all in favor of this weekly review which compels a prompt and regular appraisal of each case in the total load of his district.

The Borstal Association, like the institutions, encourages experimentation in treatment. Just before the war, for example, a parole agent found jobs for a group of Borstal lads on one project—construction of a pipe line —which it was expected would take three years to complete. With the permission of the Director thirteen ex-Borstal lads were allowed to work on the same job and live together in the nearby village. The foreman was made acquainted with the prior record of the boys and urged to take a personal interest in them. Ordinarily the Association does not believe in having even two parolees working or living together. This experiment offered such long-range possibilities, however, that it was decided to risk it, even though it ran completely contrary to established policy.

The revocation of parole can be made only by the Prison Commissioners upon the recommendation of the Borstal Association. Parole "revokees" are always sent to the Borstal wing of the Boys' Prison at Wandsworth. The procedure there and the disposition of cases have been described in an earlier chapter. Parole revocation does not necessarily mean that there has been conviction for a new offense; persistent unsatisfactory behavior on parole may bring about revocation. Only since 1936 has the Borstal Association dealt with lads again on parole whose earlier parole had been revoked. This has meant an added burden of the most difficult cases—183 in 1936, and 179 in 1937—but even so the Director of the

Association is not altogether pessimistic about the results when they have a second chance on parole. In 1938 he stated that about fifty per cent of such cases were doing well. "Revocation of license is not always the first step to failure; in many cases it has proved to be a necessary step resulting in ultimate success."

The number of parolees cared for varies from year to year: in 1936 sixteen hundred lads were actually supervised—including 818 who came into care for the first time that year and 183 after having their parole revoked. Of these 1,001 new parolees, 216 were dealt with by the London staff, 95 by the Liverpool staff, 59 were sent to sea, and 631 were supervised by 266 official Associates in various parts of England and Wales. The numbers of parolees—over 2,000 in 1938 and again in 1939—and of official Associates have been considerably increased in recent years.

CHAPTER XV

RELEASE AND AFTER-CARE

THE sentence to Borstal training is almost invariably for three years; by statute this is the maximum time that an offender can be held in a Borstal Institution without being given the chance to show what he can do on parole. The established minimum term of training is six months. Except by order of the Home Secretary, extremely rarely issued, there is no discharge possible until that minimum has been served. However, the various institutions differ in the average length of the term served—some run as high as twenty-four or twenty-six months; others release in half of that time; while only one institution, that at Hollesley Bay, has adopted the policy of a definite term of fifteen months.

The total Borstal period of control over an offender is always four years. Hence with the variations in the length of the institutional term, all the way from six months to three years, the parole period also varies greatly. It averages about two years.

Very serious deliberation is given to the question of readiness for parole. The initial discussion regarding release originates at the monthly board meeting of the entire staff of each house. Each housemaster carries the decision of his house board to the monthly institution board meeting, which acts for the entire institution as the house acts for its particular group. The institution board consists of all housemasters and deputy housemasters, the chief disciplinary officer of the institution, the medical officer, chaplain, and deputy governor, besides the governor who presides. The governor reviews the whole case, including any previous denial of discharge and the reasons for this. Any staff member may then give his opinion regarding the boy or cite his experience with him. The procedure, while businesslike, is informal and flexible. The governor takes the consensus of the group, listening to objections if there are any, and announces the final decision either to put the boy on the discharge list or to hold the case over for another month. This discharge list is then submitted by the governor to the Visiting Committee at its next meeting, since they must act formally on all releases.

After the Visiting Committee has approved his discharge, the boy is told the precise date when he will leave the institution—three months thence. The Borstal Association is then informed of the date. In the ensuing months, the housemaster must write up a summary of the case and an appraisal of the boy for the Borstal Association, the medical officer must review his medical and physical condition, the trade instructor comments on his vocational progress, and the governor adds his opinion. When the Borstal Association has received this information from the institution, one of its parole agents is sent to interview the boy, estimate his employment possibilities and family situation, and help to decide whether or not his home is suitable for his return. Plans are then started for the community supervision which will commence the day of release from the institution.

The continuity of interest afforded by the after-care association is one of the most important elements in the

Borstal process. It has earlier been noted that the Director of the Borstal Association is present at allocation
meetings and that before leaving for the institution the
boy has met with him or one of his representatives. At
least one additional visit by a Borstal Association parole
agent is made when the boy is about half through his institutional stay. It is important to emphasize that one of
these agents visits each institution once a month and that
he may be seen in regard to any matter by any boy who
tells his housemaster that he wishes "to see the man
from the Borstal Association on his next visit." Because
he is identified with the community, it is to him that the
boy may reveal worries or desires that relate to his life
outside the institution.

The Association official who visits the institution has
no authority over any feature of institutional management. He may be asked to interview the inmate's wife
or parent or a prospective employer, or to link the lad
with an outside social agency or public authority that
may help him while he is still in the institution or after
his discharge. The agent may call upon the services of
one of the social workers connected with the allocation
center for the solution of any one of these outside problems. The Borstal Association is thus seen to be the community branch of the training process; it cooperates in
arranging the extramural affairs of the inmate and pre-
pares to receive him when he is released.

One month before he is discharged, the boy receives
his civilian clothing, which he is allowed to wear on Sundays and on trips outside the institution, in order that he
may become accustomed to it again and not feel awk-

ward or ill at ease when he goes out. With characteristic care, the ready-made suits purchased in the outside market are fitted to each boy by the institution tailoring shop. Ten days before he is discharged from the institution, a letter is sent to the boy's family by the Borstal Association setting out the terms of parole and inviting their cooperation. When the lad is ready to leave, he is told by his housemaster that a chapter in his life is closed since he has completed the course of training for which he was sent to Borstal, that his concern from now on will be to make a new life for himself. The governor climaxes his personal interest in the boy when he sees him on the morning of his discharge. He inspects clothes and kit, gives him a transportation warrant and at least sufficient pocket money to meet his needs on the way to his destination. (The precise sum is determined by three factors: the distance to his home, the amount of money he had when received, the financial condition of his home. In addition, of course, he has his savings.) The governor then has his final talk with the lad to wish him well.

Those who have families fit for them to return to and relatively near the institution may be dispatched directly to their homes. The others and all who live in the London area are taken into the central office of the Borstal Association before going to their final destination. This is economically effected because all institutions have a monthly release day, at which time the bus that takes the discharged lads to the central office can bring newly allocated boys to the institution.

It is to be noted that each parolee has been assigned to an official representative in the district to which the boy is going. This staff member or Associate of the Borstal Association is already in possession of the record which sets forth the parolee's history, needs, and possibilities.

Work is found by the Association through correspondence or direct solicitation by the Director and the parole agents. The latter develop their own special resources and the lads are encouraged also to find their own jobs. (The part that the official and the voluntary Borstal Associates play in this and in other ways has been discussed in the previous chapter.) Whenever possible, an attempt is made to fit the parolee's first job to his previous training at the institution and to start him in employment which will give an opportunity for advancement. Tools and clothing are provided for boys engaged in special work and the Association stands ready to pay for club dues, tuition fees, and school books. In the London office there is a person in the staff who spends half his time securing jobs for those who wish to go to sea.

Released lads who have no family and no place to go or whose homes are not considered suitable for their care are a first charge upon the Association. Lodgings are secured for them in advance of their release, with a limit of a weekly maximum of twenty-five shillings for board and room for the first two weeks. Hostels of one type or another are ordinarily not used, because it is believed that released lads having lived under congregate conditions for quite a period need the experience of living in an ordinary household. Over a number of years the Association has built up a list of private homes located not too far from headquarters which will take boys as they are released on parole. While these homes are intended primarily for temporary care, many boys settle down in them permanently and the Association is therefore compelled constantly to seek new homes.

An interesting example of the community support and interest enlisted is that of a postman's family who provide temporary lodgings for parolees. The parents, with their son, once visited the nearby Borstal Institution on an annual field day to see a friend's son play. While there, they fell into conversation with another lad who was soon to be released. As a result of this acquaintance, they asked permission to take this lad into their home on his discharge, and after the usual investigation, this was granted. Since this temporary placement worked out well under supervision the family has continued to put their home at the Association's disposal for other parolees.

When work or lodgings are found by the Association, the employer or householder is always informed that the boy is an ex-inmate of a Borstal Institution. This is a standing rule, established to prevent later lawsuits or other difficulty. Where a parolee finds his own position or living quarters, he makes his own decision as to whether or not to reveal his previous history.

The parole agent or the official Associate meets his parolees on the average of once a fortnight during the entire period of their parole, except when they are at sea or are otherwise out of reach. In London at least, new parolees are seen every day until they have been placed in work. The Association sends an occasional letter to each boy on parole, commenting on such news as has been received about him. Parolees in the London area are encouraged to communicate at any time by mail or telephone rather than to visit the office, except when called for an interview. It is considered better to have the parole agent meet the lads outside at stated intervals or on their request than to have numbers of them appearing at the central office. When they are called in their transportation expenses are paid.

A cooperative arrangement between the Borstal Association and the police authorities has been in force since 1912. A Borstal boy—whether on parole or discharged from parole—who finds himself stranded can go to any police station in the British Isles and state that he was once at Borstal and that he is in difficulty. The police will care for him, meanwhile communicating with the Association for directions. This provision meets such situations as confront those boys who have been discharged from a ship or suddenly dropped from their jobs. The aim is to tide boys over these brief emergency periods. It is in no wise to be confused with the European practice of requiring ex-convicts to report themselves regularly to the police authorities. Boys who are lost sight of while on parole are not on this account to be arrested or otherwise taken into custody if they are found to be working. The Army and Navy will accept a boy after he has done well on parole for a year.

It is easily understandable that by reason of all this reconstructive effort the friendly relationships established between officials and parolees frequently continue beyond the parole period. Many of the young men later turn to Associates or staff members for advice, and often social contacts are maintained by visits on the part of the former parolee to his former parole official or by the latter to the young man and his family. Through all this an immense amount of information about after-careers has been collected by the Borstal Association.

PART THREE

EFFECTIVE TRAINING AND TREATMENT

CHAPTER XVI

EVALUATING THE BORSTAL SYSTEM

ANY student of reformatory methods or, for that matter, any intelligent reader will very naturally desire to know the results of the Borstal System of reformation. In particular it cannot but be of interest to compare these with figures relating to the outcome of our own reformatory methods, even with such few figures as are given in the first chapter. But fair comparisons of statistics are always difficult to make when obviously so many variables have been determining factors in the results, when the methods of gathering information are different, and when the data are not recorded in exactly the same terms. Such disparities have already led to many contradictions in figures given out concerning the after-careers of graduates of different reformatories in this country. However, for certain reasons which will appear later, the difficulties of comparing Borstal outcomes with our own best investigated reformatory results need not be regarded as overwhelming. While it is certainly much easier to show differences in the reformatory methods employed than to offer accurate comparative evaluations, nevertheless it is possible to draw some roughly valid conclusions.

It appears that no thoroughgoing, scientifically oriented study of the after-results of Borstal treatment has ever been made. But then, with the exception of the already mentioned study of Concord ex-inmates by the Gluecks, no such piece of research has been undertaken in this country. As every scientific observer in this field knows, correlations of results with types of causation of criminal tendencies and with types of treatment have to be made; otherwise a statement of results is largely meaningless. For example, there must be a considerable percentage of abnormal personalities among the Borstal population, just as there is in any diagnosed series of delinquents or criminals in this country, but no separate account of results with this group is given though we are well aware that institutional treatment for a couple of years or even longer proves of little avail in such cases for the prevention of further antisocial conduct. In the Borstal Association publications we find some statements about the varieties of abnormal human material, not certifiable as insane or mentally defective, which have to be dealt with, but as in most American statistics, the outcomes of institutional life and of parole are all lumped together.

From time to time over the years various general statements have been published. In the Borstal Association annual report for 1938 we read: "Sufficient be it to say that the majority of young men discharged from Borstal make good before the licence period has expired, and though the failures claim the headlines, as failures always will, the successes, like the majority of ordinary citizens, are not anxious for publicity. There are over 15,000 men in England today, most of them married and in their own homes, who during the last thirty years have passed through a Borstal institution." The Prison Commission report for 1936 states that on February 1,

1936, in a total male prison population of 8,462, there were only 688 (8.1 per cent) ex-Borstal lads serving sentences of imprisonment, penal servitude, or preventive detention. At that time 13,294 had graduated from Borstal training.

Before coming to more detailed figures it should be emphasized that the close-knit court, police, and penal systems of England render possible a compilation of information about the careers of offenders that is unequalled in our country. The Home Office supervises the methods of gathering and recording data which apply uniformly to every district. The Central Criminal Record Office at Scotland Yard receives from the Prison Commission data on Borstal receptions and discharges and also serves as a source of information concerning court records and reconvictions. Their records and fingerprint files are admittedly comprehensive and are constantly added to and very extensively utilized by the police all over the country. Then the Borstal Association made an arrangement in 1935 with Scotland Yard whereby beginning from that date the police report to the Association all reconvictions within five years of discharge in the case of all lads discharged from Borstal parole after January 1, 1931.

Another factor which tends to give high reliability to their own estimates of success and failure is the careful record-keeping of the Prison Commission and Borstal Association. Their data are largely obtained from parole agents and Associates who have known the lads intimately for years. When police information is added there is likely to be no large margin of error, except in the comparatively few cases of those who emigrate overseas.

Because of the above sources of information the collected data have a validity perhaps fairly comparable to that of the Massachusetts Reformatory studies made by the Gluecks.

Another outstanding reason for giving credence to the evaluations made by the Borstal Association staff and by the governors who have taken pains to collect data on their own cases is the fact, so impressed on us by personal contacts, that a frankly critical and non-defensive attitude is taken by all officials in the Borstal System.

So far as we can ascertain, the most reliable figures for evaluating recent Borstal achievement are those derived from a study made in 1939 of after-careers as related to seven institutions with their different types of training. These data, not yet published, were furnished us by the Director of the Borstal Association in September of that year. The study covers the records through 1938 of all lads discharged during the five-year period from January, 1932, through December, 1936. The time elapsed varies, then, from a minimum of two years to a maximum of seven years. The criterion for the term "success" is lack of reconviction for an offense.

But any proper interpretation of even the carefully collected data of later years involves considerations other than merely assigning percentages of success to the given institutions. In particular, questions arise about the number of lads discharged on parole from the different institutions, and whether all the institutions were in operation and releasing lads during the whole five-year period. Concerning the types of boys in each of the Borstals something has been stated in earlier chapters. We offer the following attempt to make the total figures truly meaningful.

To the North Sea Camp, established in May, 1935, is attributed 84 per cent "success." For reasons already given we should not doubt this but to the end of 1936 only 38 lads were released on parole.

The figures for Sherwood, established October, 1932, are 70 per cent "success" for the 143 who had been released by December, 1936.

The percentages of "success" reported in 1939 and the number of releases during the years 1932–1936, inclusive, for five institutions which had been fully in operation by 1931 are as follows:

	Percentage of "success"	Number of releases
Lowdham Grange	77	431
Rochester	60	815
Feltham	59	927
Camp Hill	55	759
Portland	50	958

Wandsworth, as described in Chapter XII, receives several classes of failures. Included are the few who do not conform within the training institutions and some uncontrollable absconders. These represent the incorrigible types, those who cannot or will not respond. (From what we have learned through the official reports of Borstal failures over a period of years it seems undoubtedly a fact that a sizable proportion of transferred cases are

what would be termed in this country abnormal personalities or defective delinquents.) Nevertheless, 30
per cent of the 107 released from Wandsworth during
the five-year period which the above figures cover are
reported in 1939 as "successes."

Regarding the total percentage of "success," which it
is impossible to calculate from the figures given for the
separate institutions, we may cite a statement from the
Report of the Prison Commissioners, February, 1938.
Here it is said that of the 883 graduating in 1933 from
the six Borstals then in operation, 53.6 per cent had not
been reconvicted four to five years after they had been
out, namely, at the end of December, 1937; and of the
808 released in 1935, 67.7 per cent had not been reconvicted in two to three years.

From the reports issued in 1937 and 1938 comments
on these figures are worth noting. Those discharged in
1933 came out when the employment situation was difficult and had received their training at a time when rapid
expansion was putting a great strain on the Borstal System. "The results so far of discharges in 1935–6 give
every reason to hope that with greater continuity of
control and staff the figures will show an improvement
in future years." Moreover, in many cases the reconviction occurred during the parole period, and "after a
further period of training at the Borstal Institution at
Wandsworth, the lad has been re-licensed and thereafter
has continued satisfactorily." In the 1937 report of the
Borstal Association it is stated that during 1936 there
were 183 lads who were again placed on parole after
Wandsworth. Experience shows that 50 per cent of those

placed on parole a second time ultimately succeed. If we may judge from the number who after reconviction merely had their parole revoked it is evident that comparatively few had committed offenses serious enough to warrant definite terms of imprisonment.

We may remind the reader that the age of commitment to Borstal prior to September, 1936, was sixteen to twenty-one years; also that of the boys committed all but about ten per cent had been convicted earlier and some had even served a prison sentence. For example the 1,011 lads committed in 1933 had previous convictions as follows.

Convictions	Number
None known	96
One	297
Two	264
Three	182
Four	70
Five	57
Six to ten	41
Above ten	4

The ages on conviction to Borstal in 1933 were:

16 years	119
17 years	217
18 years	205
19 years	196
20 years	117
Total	854

In any consideration of Borstal treatment or its results, it is important to bear in mind that Borstal commitments include all but the smallest handful of those within the Borstal age limits who receive a sentence of more than a year. The following table presents these figures for the years 1930–1937, inclusive:[1]

Year	Total males, 16–21, sentenced to imprisonment other than Borstal	Sentenced to 12 months or less (90% 6 months or less)	Sentenced to more than 12 months	Sentenced to Borstal	Percentage committed to Borstal, of all those sentenced to more than 12 months
1930	1872	1864	8	725	98.9
1931	1883	1850	33	873	96.4
1932	2653	2593	60	1011	94.4
1933	2253	2225	28	854	96.8
1934	1894	1878	16	793	98.0
1935	1608	1597	11	686	98.4
1936	1237	1223	14	776	98.2
1937	1275	1240	35	875	96.2
Totals	14,675	14,470	205	6593	97.0

Thus over an eight-year period Borstal received all but 205 youths between sixteen and twenty-one who were sentenced for a year or more, the commitments to Borstal being 97 per cent of the entire group.

Although the study of 1939 offers the most comprehensive and valid figures for Borstal after-careers, still it is of value to examine some of the earlier attempts to appraise results. While none of these was developed against a background of data as comprehensive as that utilized for the latest study, yet they greatly tend to increase the weight of evidence concerning outcomes. To a considerable degree the findings dovetail and substantiate one another.

1. Source: *Reports of the Prison Commissioners* for the corresponding years.

After Borstal training had been in official operation for six years, the prison authorities made the first follow-up study. This in 1915 was undertaken for 1,454 boys, all those who had been discharged between August, 1909, and March, 1914, a period of four and a half years. Though not so complete as for later studies, the criminal records for all of Great Britain and the files of the Borstal Association were the sources of information regarding these later histories of ex-Borstal lads, all of whom had been at liberty at least a year when the investigation was made. The findings were that:

940 (64.6%) have not since been reported as re-convicted, and were satisfactory when last heard of;

122 (8.4%) were unsatisfactory when last heard of, but have not been reported as re-convicted;

392 (27.0%) have been reported as re-convicted.

As might have been expected, the following figures show that those cases which had been longest released from Borstal had been reconvicted in a higher proportion than those cases which had been recently released.

Discharged during the year ending	*Percentage not reconvicted by 1915*
March 31, 1910	64.6
March 31, 1911	67.0
March 31, 1912	65.9
March 31, 1913	73.6
March 31, 1914	83.2

Used at that time as an argument for early apprehension and training of offenders was the fact that the percentage of the group who were doing well after release was in almost direct ratio to their age when they were first sent for Borstal training:

Age when committed	Percentage not reconvicted
Under 17	82.6
17 and under 18	85.3
18 and under 19	77.9
19 and under 20	77.0
20 and under 21	63.4

In 1923 the Borstal Association reported the results of a follow-up of 270 individuals released during the year ending March, 1912, all of whom had been at liberty for eleven years or more. Of these, 163 (60 per cent) had not been reconvicted.

The 1925 Association report states that of 2,089 boys who had been discharged in the five-year period ending with 1924 (of course, some of them out only for short periods), 1,474 (70 per cent) had not been again reconvicted.

In the 1928 report the statement is made that:

Of lads whose period at Borstal was their first experience of institutional treatment over seventy-one per cent have become satisfactory.

Of those who had been sent to prison before Borstal only fifty-five per cent have become satisfactory.

Of those who had been sent both to a reformatory and prison before Borstal less than forty-nine per cent made good.

The following table gives the "Position at the end of December, 1938, of lads discharged from Borstal Institutions during the three years 1934–1936."[2] This covers

2. *Report of the Prison Commissioners . . . 1939.*

a minimum of two and a maximum of five years since discharge.

Year	Total discharges from all institutions	Not since reconvicted	Reconvicted once only	Reconvicted two or more times
1934	900	524 (58.2%)	174 (19.3%)	202 (22.5%)
1935	808	505 (62.5%)	180 (22.3%)	123 (15.2%)
1936	818	574 (70.2%)	149 (18.2%)	95 (11.6%)
Total	2526	1603 (63.5%)	503 (19.9%)	420 (16.6%)

Parole revokees dealt with again on parole by the Borstal Association:

1936	. . . . .	232
1937	. . . . .	183
1938	. . . . .	179

While one sees plainly that the above appraisals are difficult to compare from a statistical standpoint, yet they do show honest and frequent efforts to evaluate results of the treatment process. A number of variables immediately come to mind which may account for differences in the recorded results. For example, the figures for earlier years cover discharges from the institutions during a period when the Borstal System was not at its present stage of development, and in the later reports, where after-careers are appraised, newer facilities and methods for reporting and recording have added to the completeness and accuracy of follow-up data.

We have made every effort to discover some method of utilizing the figures given in this chapter, and other statistics which we have at hand, for making some valid comparisons with figures on outcomes of reformatory

treatment in the United States, more particularly with
those appearing in the Gluecks' studies. But there are so
many differences in the way in which data were gathered, put together, and the findings presented that for
the most part the task of accurate comparisons seems
insuperable.

Nevertheless, any thoughtful reader who is at all accustomed to delving into the data of criminal recidivism
must find in these figures much that is interesting and
valuable as bearing on the results of Borstal training.
The small percentage of ex-Borstal lads at any given
time among the total prison population; the comparatively small number of parole revokees that, as we have
indicated earlier, have to be dealt with at Wandsworth
or by the Borstal Association; the fact that 70 per cent
are not reconvicted during a period of two years after
discharge; and the several available figures for five or
more years after discharge—all these are illuminating.

The earlier and later appraisals tend to make a consistent picture. The reports show a gradual higher rate
of reconviction as the elapsed period since release in-
creases. Also the lower the age of original commitment,
the higher was the percentage of non-criminal conduct.
Then the 1928 analysis reveals a difference of 22 per
cent in the "success" rate when a Borstal sentence was
the first institutional experience as compared with the
results when both a reformatory and a prison term had
previously been served, while the lads who had been
sent only to prison before Borstal were not reconvicted
in a percentage which lay between these extremes. That

only 30 per cent of Wandsworth cases were not reconvicted during a two to seven-year period, that 77 per
cent of 431 graduates of Lowdham Grange were "successes" according to the same criterion, while the "success" rate for other institutions ranged between these
limits in accordance with the type of offender committed
to them, add a convincing note to the general credibility
of the follow-up figures.

Leaving aside everything else it is finally possible to
come at least to one important conclusion concerning
comparisons that appear valid within a reasonably narrow margin of error.

The figures for 1938 showed for 883 individuals,
53.6 per cent of "success" as judged by no reconviction
within four to five years after discharge in 1933 from
Borstal. The 1939 figures were 58.2 per cent of "success" over a like period for 900 discharged in 1934.
These totals are more than two and a half times as great
as the 21.1 per cent of success during the five-year post-
parole period of 510 prisoners discharged from the
Massachusetts Reformatory.

Suggestive for possible interpretation of the number
of post-Borstal convictions is the fact that convictions
and sentences for minor offenses are very common in
England. In 1938, for example, 51 per cent of all the
men sentenced to prison received terms not exceeding
one month, and 88 per cent for terms not exceeding six
months. While separate recording of post-Borstal convictions or length of sentences could not be found, still
it is interesting in the light of the above figures to note

that the 44 per cent of Massachusetts Reformatory graduates who were resentenced received sentences averaging twenty-two months.

At this point it is pertinent to discuss what from our observations and prior experience seem to us possible weaknesses in the Borstal System. If these were overcome perhaps one might expect a further decrease in recidivism, even though the Borstal figures show the largest measure of favorable results from reformative treatment that appear validly established anywhere. All the critical notes which follow found some support in statements made by various members of the Borstal personnel.

In the first place, all competent scientific studies of any considerable series of offenders, young or old, have revealed a significant proportion of abnormal personalities among them. Leaving out of account the psychotic and the mentally defective, there are certain other cases, termed psychopathic personalities, constitutionally inferior personalities, post-traumatic personalities, and so on, which present extremely difficult material from a reformative standpoint.

Even among those long connected with the Borstal method of training there is a wide discrepancy in impressionistic judgments of the percentage of abnormal personalities or of any sub-class of them among Borstal inmates in general or in a given institution. One of the leading authorities suggested that if Borstal is getting good results at all with this class of cases it is due to "not making too much of their abnormality," keeping them in normal groups and fitting them into work according to their special abilities and needs. Thus one finds in the Borstal System no consistent attempt to diagnose these cases, understand their peculiarities, or determine the proportion of them among the recidivists.

The success achieved with abnormal personalities by clinics, institutions, social agencies, probation and parole officials having proven in our country to be meager indeed, the critical student of the results of the Borstal System will want to know what its experience has been with such problem cases. In any forward-looking scheme of training and treatment for offenders scientific knowledge of the types of human beings dealt with is a prerequisite to a well-planned program and to common-sense evaluation of results.

This brings up the whole matter of the application of modern psychiatry in a reformatory system. It is true, as the Borstal people say, that we in America have concerned ourselves more with psychiatric classification of offenders in institutions and with statistical researches, while the Borstal System has been devoted to experiments in treatment. But the two approaches are by no means incompatible; indeed, in a scientifically well-oriented program both are indispensable. Treatment not based on diagnosis or etiology is not in line with the effective development of therapy in medicine or any of the biological sciences. Psychiatry as applied to the study of offenders has advanced far beyond the explanation of criminality in terms of mental abnormality. Together with psychiatric social work it has revealed many of the traumatic life experiences and emotional attitudes, the feelings of being thwarted or deprived, which lead to the ready acceptance of ideas of criminality as being for the particular individual a suitable form of behavior.[3]

To be sure, as we have stated earlier, no small part of the work done with Borstal lads partakes of the nature of psychotherapy; yet it is equally true that the fine endeavor to utilize personal influence is based very largely on the subjective impressions of the individual members of the staffs. Their knowledge of the causations of human behavior is not that of the psychiatrist who patiently unearths a life story and has the opportunity of fitting it together with what a psychiatric social worker has learned with equal patience from the stories of the families. In spite of the splendid chances offered by the Borstal setting for such expert work, psychiatrists are not at hand to undertake it.

An attempt at "the psychological treatment of crime"[4] was begun in 1934, but, as might have been expected, so far as the Borstal lads were concerned since they were transferred for such treatment to a typical prison atmosphere, as well as for other reasons, the outcomes were largely unsatisfactory. However, enough was discovered to warrant a statement by the Prison Commissioners of their favorable attitude toward establishing a colony

3. To what an extent tendencies to antisocial conduct may be engendered by emotional deprivations and frustrations, particularly in family life, was brought out clearly by a research conducted for the Yale Institute of Human Relations. See *New Light on Delinquency and its Treatment*, W. Healy and A. F. Bronner, 1936.

4. *The Psychological Treatment of Crime*, by W. H. East and W. H. deB. Hubert, H. M. Stationery Office, 1939.

where under special conditions of training clinical studies and treatment of selected cases could be carried on.[5]

The records we have seen of social investigations of the cases of Borstal lads accumulate valuable but rather superficial data. For the most part untrained in social psychiatry, the investigators have largely missed the enormously important factors which interpersonal relationships within the family life represent. It is the understanding of these family relationships that has contributed so greatly to psychiatric thinking and practice during the last twenty years in our own country.

One standard regulation of the Borstal System seems to us to be open to grave criticism. This is the matter of the maximum period during which an offender can be held in an institution and on parole, which together cannot exceed four years. In certain difficult cases—perhaps abnormal personalities, or those with long-established antisocial attitudes, or those who are slow in stabilizing —the period of institutional training or of supervision on parole may not be long enough. If such individuals after being necessarily placed on parole at the end of three years (they are generally paroled in a shorter time) have their parole revoked within a few months, the remainder of the four years sometimes does not prove sufficient for reconstruction of their tendencies. Both in the interest of the possible rehabilitation of the individual and for the protection of society a more prolonged initial term of training and treatment in an institution for some cases and a much longer time on parole would appear to be highly justified. It must be apparent

5. *Report of the Prison Commissioners . . . 1939*, p. 50 ff.

—and some Borstal officials confirm this—that a break-down on parole or soon afterwards can be predicted either because of the instabilities of the lad or because the training period was too short.

While all are against a completely indeterminate sentence, several governors expressed the opinion that it would be better in a small proportion of the cases if they could keep a lad well beyond the three-year limit. The Commissioner who has been the leading spirit in the Borstal movement believes that in roughly 20 per cent of the cases a longer period of control is highly desirable. If the existing statutes were amended to permit it, surely the time limit for institutional training or for supervision on parole could be extended under the safeguard of thorough review of the case by the Commission, which is composed of highly experienced men.

All this leads us to say finally that with the splendid work done throughout the Borstal System there is a great opportunity for valuable research. This would involve much more than the mere accumulation of figures showing how many of those discharged from Borstal were or were not reconvicted. Fundamental problems could be studied, case by case, with the possibility of increasing the effectiveness of Borstal training methods and making important contributions which would aid vastly in the treatment of youthful offenders everywhere.

CHAPTER XVII

TOWARD MORE EFFECTIVE
ACCOMPLISHMENT

SOCIETY long ago decided that vengeance is not the answer to crime. Nowadays the laws under which an offender may be deprived of his liberty appear to be based on three concepts: society is protected during the period of segregation; punishment administered in this form may prove a deterrent—to others as well as to the offender; reformation may result. Present practice in this country entails the release of approximately ninety-six per cent of all those who are imprisoned, by far the most of them having served rather short sentences. Theoretically it is considered that with all of these released cases something has been done to the offender that will tend to deter or reform him. But to what extent does this actually happen?

All those who are well acquainted with the problems of recidivism which youthful criminals present realize that society's only safeguard from them must consist in so altering their outlook, attitude, and habits as to ensure their conformity to acceptable norms of behavior when they are returned to society. It is equally plain that we must face the necessity of long segregation for those offenders who, for whatever reason, cannot by any training process be brought to conform.

But whatever the plans that are made for skilled treatment for the reformable and prolonged segregation for the non-reformable, no such plans will succeed if we simply attempt to tack them on to our existing confusion of procedures and institutional practices. All the processes impinging upon the lives of convicted young offenders must first be consistently integrated. Necessary steps in this direction are exemplified by the provisions of a model enactment which is outlined later in this chapter.

As our reformatory systems function at present they embody certain faults which militate seriously against desirable reconstruction of behavior tendencies. Among these are the following matters:

Most of the institutions are so large that mass treatment of the inmates is necessary. The fewer the exceptions to the general daily schedule—whether for personal interviews, special activities, special instruction, or anything else—the more smoothly will the institution run, or appear to run. The rigid routine tends to kill initiative on the part of both officials and inmates. In such sterile conditions the idea that reformation requires a highly individualized approach cannot take root.

The non-working hours, for example, during evenings, Saturday afternoons, and Sundays, present a dangerous vacuum in which only too often highly undesirable thoughts and practices are engendered. The obstacles to supplying opportunities for wholesome interests and occupations during these times are almost insuperable in a typical large reformatory.

The institutions themselves are rarely limited to the age group for which reformative procedures may most profitably be adapted. Frequently there is crowding and little chance for separation of types of offenders, particu-

larly for the purpose of reducing the liability of bad influences or in accord with the needs for individualized
treatment.

Then so far as release is concerned, the usual provisions of a minimum and maximum term in an otherwise
indeterminate sentence bring about difficulties related to
the time limits set. By reason of these and various parole
requirements, such as having a job, an inmate may be
held far beyond the period when he is most fit to return
to society. On the other hand, many serious offenders
who are sure to continue in criminality are turned loose
because their "time" has been served.

The greatest weakness of our reformatories lies in the
lack of opportunities for personally influencing the offender. The custodial level at which they mainly operate attracts to the service, in any capacity, few men who
have the character, training, and outlook necessary for
re-forming careers.

Furthermore the whole mechanized regime almost
necessitates the depersonalization of the offender. Indeed the mass spirit so prevails, even among the inmates, that if a member of the staff were to introduce an
element of personal interest in some individual, both
staff and inmates would be prone to look askance at such
overtures. The tone of impersonal "democracy" must be
maintained; no one must be treated differently from his
fellows.

We see all these obstacles to the application of a fundamental principle essential to reformation, namely,
"That someone should come to know and to understand
the man in so intimate and friendly a way that he comes

to a better understanding of himself and a truer compre-
hension of the world he lives in."[1]

How different the Borstal System is in its formulation
of sound principles and in its flexible application of what
has been learned through long years of practical experiment we have endeavored to make clear through the details given in earlier chapters. Here we may recapitulate.

The age group selected for Borstal training covers the
years when the prospect of reformation is most hopeful,
and when from the standpoint of society it is most important to deal with serious offenders for the purpose of
checking criminal careers. On account of the utter reasonableness of Borstal methods and their proved measure of success the upper age for commitment has been
raised from twenty-one to twenty-three years.

From the time of sentence to Borstal detention, the
whole point and purpose of the Borstal System is in evidence. The approach to the offender from that moment
bespeaks appreciation of the fact that here is an individual who needs to be trained in the practices of social living. Not depersonalized by a set penalty inflicted for a
given act, he is regarded as someone who for the protection of society as well as for his own good should be
dealt with by thoroughgoing reconstructive methods.
The law takes charge of him in order that he may be
trained to do better than he has done for himself and
society.

It is common-sense knowledge that youthful offenders differ tremendously in their individual capacities and

1. Richard C. Cabot, Introduction to *Five Hundred Criminal
Careers*, Sheldon and Eleanor Glueck, 1930.

characteristics, and in their needs for disciplinary treatment and special forms of training, education, and up-building. This is the reason for the well-rounded study of each offender during a month of observation at the collecting center, after which a tentative diagnosis of his possibilities is made and he is allocated to one of the several available types of institutions. The procedure represents an objective and equitable method of dealing with the individual. Thus for Borstal commitments the varieties of sentencing policies of different judges are replaced by a plan based on carefully conducted investigations.

Then comes the utilization of a wealth of treatment devices which challenge the offender to build up new strengths, values, and capacities for coping with his outside environment as an honest citizen. Through a most arduous program of physical and vocational training, education, and recreation, the aim is to develop in the inmate feelings of worth and adequacy that will send him forth sure-footed into the world.

The immense importance of understanding the offender as an individual and the bearing of such understanding upon those interpersonal relationships which within the institution are stressed as an aid in his up-building receive emphasis throughout the entire period of detention. The working staff is encouraged not only to give thought to his day-by-day adjustments to institutional life but also to consider his future career. The community contacts that are such a unique feature of the Borstal program, contacts that are so markedly increased just prior to release, are deliberately planned to further the probabilities of success outside. Indeed, the whole scheme of preparation for release, with the part that the inmate takes in such preparation, is an outstanding example of the consideration that is given to his ultimate welfare.

Neither the development of such plans of training and treatment nor the carrying of them out could have been possible without attracting to the service a capable and devoted, almost consecrated, personnel. That the leaders have been able to draw such a fine body of people to work with them in many capacities is one of the most remarkable things about the Borstal System. Its success has been entirely dependent upon this.

Through the parole period, which is frequently spoken of as the after-care period, the continuity of the plan of treatment extends. The parole agency, the Borstal Association, maintains close contacts with the institutions and inmates and has educated a wide public to become interested in parolees, to accept them, and be helpful to them.

Unquestionably the results of the Borstal System are relatively much better than those obtained by the reformatories of this country. Taking into account the intelligent and continuous effort displayed in the development of this system we would naturally query, why should this not be true? No overwhelming argument can be made that the young lawbreakers sentenced to Borstal training are essentially different from the human material committed to our own reformatories. Of course social, economic, and political differences between the United States and Great Britain must bring about some contrasts in the incidence and character of youthful crime, as well as in the possibilities of working with young offenders, but still the psychology of human nature is everywhere the same. And it is just human nature, with its assets and liabilities, that has to be dealt with in the reformative process.

Features of the Borstal System are present in a few of our training schools for juveniles, but save for the outstanding example of Annandale they are almost entirely absent from the procedures of the reformatories of the United States. The results of the Borstal System prove the value of extending to the reformatory age group certain principles—such as assignment to institutional units on the basis of studies of the individual, the application of a variety of treatment methods, and belief in the utilization of personal influence—theoretically accepted by juvenile correctional institutions but very meagerly applied.[2]

After long and intensive deliberation by its specially appointed committee, a plan for dealing more effectively with youthful criminality has recently been recom-

2. For intimate studies of the treatment programs of five representative correctional institutions for boys and careful investigations of the after-careers of inmates we may refer to two publications by the Federal Children's Bureau: "Institutional Treatment of Delinquent Boys," Parts I and II. An extended survey of such institutions in many states has been made by staff members of the Osborne Association and reported on in its *Handbook of American Institutions for Delinquent Juveniles:* vol. I, 1938; vols. II and III, 1940. Osborne Association, 114 East 30th St., New York City.

mended by the American Law Institute.[3] The essentials as applicable under the laws of any given state are these: If a person over the juvenile court age and under twenty-one is convicted of an offense for which he could not merely be fined, he must be committed to an administrative body which shall take control of the offender and render a decision about what shall be done with him. In the draft of a model enactment a treatment board, tentatively named the Youth Correction Authority, is constituted as a branch of the state government.

It is contemplated that the Authority shall be composed of several highly qualified and experienced members who shall "represent legal and administrative ability, educational experience and experience in the study of youthful offenders and in planning corrective training and treatment for such offenders."

This Authority shall be furnished the facts relating to the cases and will proceed to study the offender and the pertinent circumstances of his life. As the result of such investigations he will either be placed on probation or sent to an institution for training and treatment. The probation and parole services and the institutional facilities which may be established or utilized will be under the control of the Authority. Existing public and private agencies and resources may be drawn upon; new facilities are to be created only when needs cannot otherwise

3. Copies of the official draft of the Youth Correction Authority Act adopted at the annual meeting of the American Law Institute, May, 1940, can be obtained at the offices of the Institute, 3400 Chestnut St., Philadelphia.

be met. The Authority shall have the duty of employing personnel qualified to make its investigations and to administer its training and treatment program.

Persons committed to the Authority before eighteen years of age shall be discharged from its control before the age of twenty-one, and all others shall be discharged within three years unless, in either case, the Authority has made an order stating that in the interest of public welfare the person remain longer under its control and makes application to an upper court for a determining review of that order. Thereafter at intervals new applications for review may be made. Studies of each case at least every two years is a definite requirement in order that the interests of the individual be safeguarded. In no instance can anyone be held beyond the age of twenty-five without a special review of the case and a special court order.

The provisions of the model Act with its various details are calculated to ensure the application of much more reasonable and scientific methods of training and treatment than at present obtain through sentences to prison and reformatory or through the ordinary placing of offenders on probation. The proviso, "The Authority shall keep written records of all examinations and of the conclusions predicated thereon," carries the definite implication that a research attitude shall be maintained by the Authority in relation to all the facts it gathers and particularly for evaluations of results.

This Act leaves the processes of arrest, prior detention, prosecution, and trial precisely as they function now under the criminal law of the state.[4] But after conviction, except in cases where discharge or a fine is ordered, it is the function of the constituted treatment board or Authority to determine what shall be done with the offender.

The Authority has the opportunity to plan a highly individualized method of treatment suitable to the needs of the offender and to the protection of the public. The prolonged segregation that is essential for certain cases is amply provided for, equally with the possibility of quick discharge from control when the case justifies it. All rights of appeal are covered.

This whole plan is not revolutionary; indeed it finds precedent in the social philosophy and legal procedure applied now to the juvenile offender. In most states children may be committed to the control of correctional institutions until they reach the age of twenty-one, and consequently they may remain under such control for many years—with no provision for a court review of

4. A further project of the American Law Institute was the drafting of a Youth Court Act to prevent the well-known inimical influences which bear upon a young offender through the conditions to which he is subjected between the time of arrest and conviction or discharge from temporary custody. These conditions particularly as set forth in "Youth in the Toils" are matters for great concern in many places. They can be remedied only through establishing proper places of detention and more expeditious and better methods of prosecution and trial. To this end a model enactment for the creation of "a youth court of special personnel and limited jurisdiction for metropolitan and large urban centers" has been tentatively drafted by the Institute's special committee, though it has not yet been considered for recommendation by the Institute itself.

their cases. Then in several states statutory enactments permit certain types of incorrigible or abnormal offenders to be held in preventive detention over long periods until they are considered no longer a menace to society.

But more than anything else this new plan embodied in the Youth Correction Authority Act provides for dealing wisely and effectively with youthful wrongdoers for the purpose of rehabilitating as many of them as possible through re-educative measures in order to forestall their persistence in antisocial conduct. The twin and inseparable goals of the Act are reformation of the offender and protection of society.

It will readily be appreciated that the strongest features of the Borstal System can be incorporated in the training and treatment program of the Youth Correction Authority. The intelligent methods of allocation, the opportunities for educational and vocational advancement, the arduous schedule for physical and character upbuilding, all will be possible if the three or more members of the Authority are chosen for their competence and they, in turn, enlist the services of able staff members. The consistency that will be brought about by the integration of all the services under one board will be a tremendous advantage.

The costs may be somewhat greater than at present, but no expensive buildings or elaborate equipment in addition to what our reformatories already provide are contemplated, nor should they be necessary—any more than they are under the Borstal System. The higher success rates that undoubtedly can be obtained will amply justify some early increase in per capita expenditures; the total costs of dealing with our criminal population should be markedly reduced as the program develops.

The several weaknesses that we have observed in the Borstal System and discussed in the preceding chapter can be largely eliminated under the proposed plan of training and treatment. The much more widespread utilization of psychiatric knowledge and application of the understanding of causes which derives from professional social work would lead to more accurate diagnoses and for some cases to more skilled therapeutic adjuncts to the general treatment process. The acknowledged errors that have been made during the experimental development of the Borstal method can be known and avoided. For example, through the provisions of the Authority Act it will be possible to retain under control those who, recognized as continuing menaces to society, are necessarily released by the Borstal authorities.

The prime requisite for the success of any such program as that presented in the Youth Correction Authority Act will not be found in the machinery of its organization, though the legal and administrative functioning of such a scheme is extremely important. The determining factor will prove to be the caliber of the men of all ranks who operate the machinery. The essential task of the reformative process is that of influencing human beings through the man-to-man relationships that inevitably are involved.

It would seem that our sketch of the situation in American reformatories and the details we have given of the working methods of the Borstal System surely demonstrate that a most carefully selected expert personnel is a fundamental necessity both in the central Authority and the staffs of the various branches and units that will work under it. It may be asked where the right people are to be found.

The difficulty in the past has been that a combination of political factors and a low level of correctional practice have discouraged able young persons from entering the field. But the fact that in the federal prison service and in the departments of correction in a few progressive states there are now well-qualified workers with professional attitudes proves that capable people can be attracted to such service. It is to be expected that the establishment in any state of a Youth Correction Authority with finely qualified members will draw the kind of people who are equipped to do good work and derive satisfaction from it. It should be as possible here as in the Borstal System to recruit the right men.

In the colleges and professional schools of the country there is certainly no shortage of stalwart young men with ideals, at least some of whom are nowadays asking what opportunities there are for public service. Our schools of social work are annually turning out men and women trained to enter the field of corrective treatment. And others without such training have the talents, the experience, and the point of view that would enable them to contribute greatly to the initiation of more effective practices in the rehabilitation of youthful offenders. Surely the enlistment of the services of such people waits only on the establishment of opportunities for a satisfying career.

SELECTED BIBLIOGRAPHY

1895–1938 Annual Reports of the Prison Commissioners, Home Office, London.

1904–1938 Annual Reports of the Borstal Association, 131 Victoria Street, London.

1921 E. Ruggles-Brise: The English Prison System, London, especially pp. 85–100, 118–122, 238–265.

A history of the Borstal System by the man who was Chairman of the Prison Commission at the time of the establishment of the first Borstal Institution. Contains a statement of Borstal aims, and statistics for the year 1918. The appendix contains a copy of the Prevention of Crime Act, 1908, and the Criminal Justice Administration Act, 1914, as well as instructions of the Chairman of the Prison Commission to the Governors of Borstal Institutions for carrying out the provisions of these acts.

1922 S. Hobhouse and A. F. Brockway: English Prisons To-day, London, especially pp. 298–300, 410–440.

A brief discussion of the history, population, buildings, staff, régime, industrial training, the Borstal Association, treatment of girl offenders, and statistics. Eleven criticisms of the system are offered.

1927 Report of the Departmental Committee on the Treatment of Young Offenders, H. M. Stationery Office, London.

1930 The Borstal Associate's Handbook, Borstal Association, London.

1932 The Principles of the Borstal System, Prison Commission, Home Office, London.

J. W. Gordon: Borstalians, London.

A rather glorified "public school" description of Borstal training, by one who spent a period of training in Borstal as a convicted offender.

1933 A. Rodgers: A Borstal Experiment in Vocational Guidance, British Journal of Educational Psychology, vol. 3, pp. 127–141.

A preliminary account of an experiment under the auspices of the National Institute of Industrial Psychology, in which several performance and aptitude tests were administered to boys at Borstal. On the basis of these results, an attempt at vocational guidance was made at the Borstal Institutions.

1934 S. Barman: The English Borstal System, London.

The law governing commitment to Borstal Institutions, their regulations, with some description of those then in operation, and an account of the Borstal Association; by an East Indian lawyer.

L. W. Fox: The Modern English Prison, London, especially Chapter XVI.

1935 A Borstal Experiment in Vocational Guidance (Industrial Health Research Board Report No. 78), H. M. Stationery Office, London. Final report.

1937 W. Strube: Sonderheft über das Borstal System, Blätter für Gefängniskunde, vol. 68, no. 3, Heidelberg.

1938 Criminal Justice, A Bill presented to the House of Commons by the Home Secretary, H. M. Stationery Office, London.

Borstal Regulations, Prison Commission, Home Office, London.

1939 Report of the Royal Commission in Canada to Investigate the Penal System, King's Printer, Ottawa.

Contains an account of the Borstal System with recommendations for its adoption in Canada.

1940 The English Criminal Justice Bill, Columbia Law Review, vol. 40, pp. 105–126.

A statement of the main features of this Bill.

Margaret Fry: The Borstal System, pp. 127–151 in Radzinowicz and Turner, Penal Reform in England, London.

INDEX